CAREERS IN THE MEDIA

LORETO GRAMMAR SCHOOL
OMAGH

THE KOGAN PAGE GUIDE TO CAREERS IN THE MEDIA

Edited by
Julia Allen

Copyright © Kogan Page 1989

All rights reserved. No reproduction, copy or transmission of this publication may be made without written permission.

No paragraph of this publication may be reproduced, copied or transmitted save with written permission or in accordance with the provisions of the Copyright Act 1956 (as amended), or under the terms of any licence permitting limited copying issued by the Copyright Licensing Agency, 7 Ridgmount Street, London WC1E 7AE.

Any person who does any unauthorised act in relation to this publication may be liable to criminal prosecution and civil claims for damages.

First published in Great Britain in 1989 by
Kogan Page Limited, 120 Pentonville Road,
London N1 9JN

British Library Cataloguing in Publication Data

The Kogan Page guide to careers in the media.
  1. Great Britain. Mass media –
Career guides
I. Allen, Julia
302.2'34'02341

ISBN 1-85091-668-3

Typeset by DP Photosetting, Aylesbury, Bucks
Printed and bound in Great Britain by
Biddles Limited, Guildford

Contents

Acknowledgements 6
Introduction 7
Abbreviations Used 15
1. Broadcasting 17
2. Film and Video Industries 35
3. Theatre 46
4. Performers 55
5. Journalism 71
6. Publishing 82
7. Printing 96
8. Writing 104
9. Advertising 110
10. Public Relations 117
11. Marketing 121
12. Artist and Illustrator 131
13. Design 137
14. Photography 142
15. Arts Administration and Sponsorship Work 149
16. Agency Work 154
17. Information Gathering and Handling 161
18. Administration and Back-up Work 168
Index 173

Acknowledgements

For much of the information in this book I am indebted to current Kogan Page titles, and have made use of material from the following: *Careers in Art and Design* by Linda Ball, *Careers in Film* by Ricki Ostrov, *Careers in Journalism* by Peter Medina and Vivien Donald, *Careers in Photography* by David Higgs, *Careers in Publishing* by June Lines, and *Careers in the Theatre* by Jean Richardson.

I should like to thank the following individuals and institutions for the information they provided: Anne Rawcliffe-King, Training Officer, ACTT, the Arts Council, Book House Training Centre, British Actors Equity Association, the Home Office, the Industrial Marketing Research Association, the Institute of Marketing, the Market Research Society, the Newspaper Society, Regional Theatre Young Director Scheme, Janet Greco, Training Officer, Super Channel. My unfailingly patient and encouraging commissioning editor at Kogan Page, who drew my attention to a lot of interesting and useful material. Michael Minden and David Wilcockson taught me to use my word processor, without which this book would never have been produced on time.

Introduction

This book offers factual information about job opportunities in the media today. The mass media are, of course, the means of communication that reach large numbers of people – newspapers, magazines, radio, television and advertisements etc – but the scope of the book is wider than this. No one chapter is self-contained; all are extensively cross-referenced and lead the reader into other related fields. A few examples will illustrate how closely interconnected media jobs are. A mass circulation consumer magazine generates work for journalists, artists, photographers, designers, editors, printers, advertising executives, marketing and sales staff; a broadcasting organisation will employ news staff who may have a print journalism background and actors who will also work in films and on the stage; the actors who appear on the screen or stage will, very probably, employ an agent to find them work; agents also market the work of writers and arrange assignments for models, artists and photographers; photographers do a lot of work for advertising agencies, which in turn employ copywriters who may also write television commercials. And so it goes on in ever-widening interlocking circles. As a user of the book you should start where you think your interests lie and see where this takes you; with luck it may be into areas you had not thought of exploring.

Each chapter gives a general description of the work or different jobs in the field; the job opportunities, eg whether jobs are available all over the country or just in the London area, the state of the job market (expanding, static or contracting), where the jobs are advertised etc; the career development you might expect, though in media jobs this is difficult to predict; the personal qualities needed for this kind of work; minimum starting salaries (where the information is available or relevant); information on union membership and/or equal opportunities (where relevant); entry requirements and training; courses, awards, professional bodies and sources of further information. When you find an area of work that interests you, you should try to look at some of the suggested further reading (many of the titles will be available in a public library), send for college prospectuses, write to the professional bodies and recruitment officers of companies. This book is only a starting point; it will, for example, give you no insight into what it is like doing any of the jobs described; for that you should turn to the books in the Kogan Page 'Careers in' series. These contain 'case studies', interviews with people in posts who talk about their work and tell you about the realities behind the recruiting literature.

Job Opportunities

You do not have to move to London in order to find a job in the media. Admittedly, the national newspapers, the BBC (Broadcasting House), many of the larger publishing firms and the biggest advertising agencies are in London, but journalists train with a provincial or local paper; there is a country-wide network of local radio stations and 15 regional television companies; lists of advertising agencies and design consultancies can be seen in every volume of the Yellow Pages; companies in all corners of the UK need public relations officers or marketing staff; most provincial towns contain a printing works and a photography business; writers can work anywhere they choose to set up their table and typewriter; and colleges of further and higher education are within easy travelling distance of most people. All this means that you can train, gain work experience, build up contacts and perhaps buy your first house in an area where you are not up against the toughest competition and the highest prices.

Employee or Freelance?

When you are at the beginning of your career it is a good idea to look for a salaried post as it is reassuring to have a sum of money coming in each month. However, there is almost no salaried work for performers so if you are an aspiring performer it is prudent to develop another skill, eg typing, switchboard operating, cocktail shaking, that enables you to earn a living between acting or concert engagements.

Many people in the media work freelance – some from choice, some from necessity – and the going can be very tough to begin with. If you are making the transition from salaried to freelance status, plan the move carefully; build up as wide a network of contacts as you can, assemble a portfolio (or other evidence) of your best work, consider employing an agent and an accountant, find out from the DHSS what your rights and obligations are, and take advice on such matters as insurance and pension plans. (See *Working for Yourself: The Daily Telegraph Guide to Self-Employment* published by Kogan Page.)

You have to be completely reliable about such things as deadlines when you work freelance and it is very easy to take on too much, or the wrong sort of work, because you are afraid to turn down a job and risk losing a potentially useful contact, or because you are worried about not making enough money.

Finding Work

Media jobs are advertised in such specialised publications as *The Stage* and in the so-called 'quality press' – *The Times, Daily Telegraph, Independent, Sunday Times, Observer* and, most useful of all, Monday's *Guardian*. Competition for advertised posts is always intense and there is something to be said for writing on spec to potential employers. Whatever your approach, you are going to have to prepare a curriculum vitae (CV) and it is very important that your CV and letter of application make a good impression because media employers receive hundreds – in the case of the BBC, thousands – of letters.

Letter of Application
At the risk of stating the obvious, here are some guidelines:

- Make a rough draft of your letter of application and check that it contains all essential points.
- It does not matter if you cannot type your letter, but it must be neat and legible.
- Use good quality, preferably white, writing paper and a matching envelope.
- Address the letter to the Head of Appointments or Chief Personnel Officer or Head of Recruiting Department (or some other such person).
- If you know this person's name (you may have seen it in a brochure or leaflet), *use it*. If you write 'Dear Mr/Ms So-and-so' sign off 'Yours sincerely'; if you do not know the name write 'Dear Sir or Madam' and sign off 'Yours faithfully'.
- Type or print your name under your signature.
- If you have any doubts about spelling or grammar show your letter

to a teacher or tutor or a reliable friend or relative (it is probably a good idea to do this in any case).
- Keep a copy of your letter for reference.
- If you are replying to an advertisement, say where you saw it.

Find out all you can about the organisation you are applying to: what are its products/programmes, who are its readers/users/audience/consumers? Be specific about your own interests, skills and experience. It is not enough simply to say that you would like a job in publishing/advertising/local radio. You must give your reasons. Keep your letter short and make your CV as comprehensive as possible.

Curriculum Vitae
Type your CV (or have it typed) if you possibly can. It is worth paying to have a CV typed professionally (keep the master and make photocopies); a good typist will know how to set it out and might be able to advise on content and phrasing. A CV should include:

- Full name and address.
- Date of birth.
- Schools attended.
- Examinations passed (dates and grades).
- Any other honours won at school or college.
- Any particular position of authority held at school, eg school captain.
- Training courses/colleges attended and qualifications gained (dates and grades).
- Previous jobs held or any other experience (names of employers and dates).
- Names and addresses of two referees. One of these should be a previous employer or someone who has personal knowledge of your abilities.
- Personal interests and hobbies, especially those relevant to the job you would like.
- Foreign languages – indicate your level of competence (eg, do you speak/write/read the language?).
- Driving licence. A clean current driving licence is needed for many jobs; if you have one, mention it.

The Interview
You may feel very nervous at an interview and find it difficult to collect your thoughts when asked even quite simple and obvious questions. It is

a good idea to think out what you would say in answer to these questions:

- Why do you want a career in journalism/advertising/publishing (or whatever the area is)?
- What made you apply for this particular job/write to this organisation?
- Why do you think you will be good at this job/you have something to offer this organisation?
- What attracts you to this job/organisation?
- How much do you know about this organisation?
- How would you like your career to develop/What would you like to be doing in five/ten years' time?
- (If you already have a job) Why do you want to leave your present job?

Remember that you will be competing for work in an area where flair and proven commitment count for more than qualifications. A degree or recognised diploma will open a few doors, but in the eyes of a potential employer they may well count for less than a portfolio of your published articles, drawings, design work or photographs, a film script or film/video footage, or a demo tape. Everyone has to start somewhere and, of course, employers do not imagine that work experience is the only proof of ability and interest; they will want to know about your involvement in such things as hospital or campus radio, amateur theatricals (on the stage or behind the scenes), school or college publications. They will expect you to show some knowledge of the area you are trying to break into; for example, if you are seeking work in an advertising agency, you should be able to talk about the most interesting current television commercials, about particular newspaper and magazine advertisements, about recent government campaigns. You will have to convince your interviewers that you are fascinated by advertising and not give the impression that you might toss off a little copy while finishing your novel.

Union Membership

There has been a tradition of powerful unions in the media: Equity, the Musicians' Union, the Association of Cinematograph, Television and Allied Technicians, the National Union of Journalists and the print unions. In some areas a closed shop still operates, but changes have taken, and are taking, place and it is impossible to say how the situation will develop. If you are planning to seek work in journalism, broadcasting, the film, video or printing industries, or as a performer, you should write to the relevant union to find out what the current membership regulations are.

Equal Opportunities

Most employers in the UK announce the fact that they are equal opportunities employers, while (consciously or unconsciously) practising sexual, racial and other kinds of discrimination. It is an indisputable fact that the majority of top media jobs are held by able-bodied, white, middle-class men. When vested interests are at stake change comes about slowly, but it is beginning. The BBC is currently running a course exclusively for Asian and Afro-Caribbean trainee reporters and presenters and the Independent Media Training Trust (89a Kingsland High Street, London E8 2PB) has been launched in order to train ethnic minority technicians for production work.

Career Development

In some areas, eg advertising, those with talent and ideas can rise very rapidly and make a great deal of money. In other areas, eg the film industry, you could spend years as a runner before getting your first break. Wherever you work you will have to cope with stiff competition and be able to perform well under pressure. The chances are that you will change jobs/ sectors several times. A journalist, after training in the provinces, could move to London then branch out into television or financial PR. A copywriter could move into writing scripts for commercials and progress from there to film scripts. A publishing house employee may end up running a literary agency. A PR executive might become interested in sponsorship work and cross over into arts management. There are endless possibilities and experience gained in one field will equip you to work in another.

Personal Qualities

Any newspaper, radio station, television company, advertising agency or publishing house will have on its staff people with widely differing characters and talents. There is no typical media employee. However, it is possible to make one or two generalisations. Media jobs are much sought after. In order to get one, therefore, you will have to be better than average at what you do (be this copywriting or bookkeeping). Many jobs, especially in journalism and broadcasting, involve long unsocial working hours so you must be 100 per cent committed and able to prove this. Media work often has to be done to a deadline and can, for this reason, be stressful. Do you perform well under pressure? Scores of people are involved in bringing out a newspaper, making a television commercial/film/radio programme, putting on a concert, running a festival, planning an advertising/PR campaign. Are you a good team member? That is to say, can you be relied upon to play your part (however small) competently and produce your work on time? Do not imagine that you have to be creative in order to get a media job; there are, of course, wonderful opportunities for creative people, but newspaper editors, for example, rate factual accuracy above imagination. There are also a great many administrative, back-up and technical posts for which professional competence and technical expertise are needed and which make interesting and satisfying careers.

Entry Requirements and Training

In order to practise certain jobs outlined in this book, eg library and information work, newspaper journalism and press photography, you have to acquire professional qualifications. In other fields, eg art and design, it is highly desirable to undergo professional training. There are also certain recognised professional qualifications, eg the CAM Certificate or Diploma, the possession of which may improve your career prospects. If you are in any doubt about qualifications and training, write to one of the professional bodies or trade unions, or to the employer for whom you would like to work. Before you enrol on a course, make sure that it will lead to a relevant, recognised/accredited qualification.

Degree Courses

Many media employers, eg the BBC, advertising agencies, PR consultancies, recruit graduate trainees, but rarely stipulate in which discipline your degree should be. Obviously, some subjects are more relevant to certain jobs than others. There are a number of media studies degree courses, but these are not necessarily the best ones to take if you want to work in the media; an arts, social sciences or psychology degree would be equally useful.

The minimum requirements for admission to a degree course are five GCSE/GCE passes, including English language, of which two must be at A level, or five SCE passes, including English, of which three must be at H grade. Occasionally, BTEC/SCOTVEC qualifications are acceptable. There is a great demand for university and polytechnic places and you will certainly need more than the minimum qualifications. Check details in the prospectus of the university or polytechnic in which you are interested. You apply for a place through the Universities Central Council on Admissions (UCCA), PO Box 28, Cheltenham, Gloucestershire GL50 IHY or the Polytechnics Central Admissions System (PCAS), PO Box 67, Cheltenham, Gloucestershire GL50 3AP.

GCE O Levels, A Levels, CSE and GCSE

The General Certificate of Secondary Education (GCSE) syllabuses and examinations have now replaced O levels and the CSE in all parts of the UK except Scotland. The new certificates are graded A to G and grades A to C are equivalent to O level grades A to C and CSE grade 1. As most of the users of this book will hold O levels the formula 'O levels (or equivalent)' has been used throughout. Please check with a careers teacher/officer, university admissions officer or potential employer if you are in any doubt about the equivalence of your qualifications.

Further information will be found in *British Qualifications* (Kogan Page), the *Handbook of Degree and Advanced Courses* (National Association of Teachers in Further and Higher Education), CRAC *Graduate Studies* (Hobsons Press), and CRAC *Directory of Further Education* (Hobsons Press). Careers information – particularly information on training, courses, entry requirements, colleges etc – rapidly becomes out of date so please check details at source.

Julia Allen
1988

Abbreviations Used

A level	Advanced level (GCE)
ACTT	Association of Cinematograph, Television and Allied Technicians
A&D	Art and Design
BA	Bachelor of Arts
BSc	Bachelor of Science
BTEC	Business and Technician Education Council
C	College
CA	College of Art
CAD	College of Art and Design
CF&HE	College of Further and Higher Education
CFE	College of Further Education
CHE	College of Higher Education
CNAA	Council for National Academic Awards
CSE	Certificate of Secondary Education
GCE	General Certificate of Education
GCSE	General Certificate of Secondary Education
H grade	Higher grade (SCE)
HNC	Higher National Certificate
Hons	Honours
IHE	Institute of Higher Education
MA	Master of Arts
MSc	Master of Science
NC	National Certificate
O level	Ordinary Level (GCE)
Poly	Polytechnic
SCE	Scottish Certificate of Education
SCOTVEC	Scottish Technical and Vocational Education Council
TC	Technical College
U	University

Chapter 1
Broadcasting

The Jobs

Broadcasting – television and radio – is a vast field; it employs thousands of people doing a wide range of jobs. The job descriptions that follow could have been divided into radio and television jobs and grouped under such headings as artistic, administrative etc. However, that would have been unsatisfactory because many jobs are common to both media and many call for creativity *and* a high degree of technical competence, or for administrative *and* artistic expertise. The simple, though not ideal, solution that has been adopted is to present the jobs in alphabetical order. Anyone using this book will realise the obvious fact that camera crews and make-up artists are not employed in radio, and readers interested in, say, library work or sound recording will realise that careers are open to them in both radio and television. A number of the jobs available in television and radio, eg actor, scene painter, are also available in other fields, such as the film industry or the theatre, and readers are referred to places in the book where these jobs are described.

Accountancy, Administration (see Chapter 18)

Announcer
Announcers (sometimes known as continuity announcers) provide the links between and within programmes. They also, to a great extent, project the company's image, so the various companies will be looking for widely differing kinds of people. However, all announcers, whether they have a regional accent or received pronunciation (standard English), need a well-modulated voice, a warm friendly personality and, for television, a pleasant appearance. The job, with its aura of glamour, is one of the most sought after in broadcasting, but there is more to announcing than introducing or trailing (giving advance information about) a programme. Many announcers write their own continuity material and if there is a technical hitch the announcer has to ad lib to fill an awkward gap. The work may include interviewing, reading

scripted commentaries, 'filler' pieces, news bulletins and news flashes etc. Most announcers have had an A level or university education and some speech training or theatrical experience. Vacancies are usually for trainee announcers.

Audio Work (see **Sound Operator**, p 25)

Camera Operator
Two kinds of camera are used in television: electronic cameras and film cameras. The use of electronic cameras is increasing, particularly of the light-weight electronic news-gathering (ENG) camera. It is not difficult for those who have acquired film camera skills to transfer them to the electronic camera. (See also p 38.)

Carpenter and Joiner (see p 51)

Clerk (see p 170)

Continuity (see p 37)

Costume Designer
Costume designers work in the areas of television light entertainment and drama. They begin by reading the programme script, then, in liaison with the producer, director, choreographer and set designer, plan the costumes and work out the costume budget. Costume designers should have a good grounding in the history of costume and etiquette and be creative and innovative while possessing administrative and supervisory skills. Some television companies have their own stock of costumes, others rely on theatrical costumiers. One of the entry points to the profession is as *costume design assistant*. The assistant's duties include arranging fittings, doing research and shopping for fabrics and accessories. Applicants normally hold a degree or equivalent qualification in theatrical or fashion design and have had professional experience in, for example, the theatre. (See also **Designer**, p 48.)

Craft Posts (see p 51)

Data Processing (see p 169)

Disc Jockey/DJ (see **Music Presenter**, p 21)

Director (see **Programme Director**, p 23)

Dresser
Dressers are responsible for the maintenance of costumes and for helping artistes on and off with their costumes. They carry out minor alterations and must therefore be able to sew quickly and neatly. They need tact and sensitivity when dealing with artistes. Both men and women can work as dressers, but people who are under the age of 20 are rarely recruited as dressers. (See also **Wardrobe Staff**, p 52.)

Dressmaker
Dressmakers work on any kind of costume from a caveman's skin to a martian's spacesuit and are expected to make their own patterns from the designer's working drawings. A dressmaker will have had basic training in pattern-making, cutting and dressmaking to BTEC HND level and work experience as a proven dressmaker or with a fashion house or theatrical costumier (see also **Wardrobe Staff**, p 52).

Editor – Videotape, ENG
As most television programmes are recorded on videotape, there is a great demand for videotape editors. The tape is contained on reels and when edit points have been decided the sections of the tape to be used in the production are recorded on to another tape. Editing machines are complicated pieces of equipment but relatively easy to learn to operate; it is not necessary to have a technical background in order to become a videotape editor.

ENG editors use the same techniques as videotape editors but work with small cassettes rather than large reels. They have to meet deadlines for news bulletins and are usually working under great pressure. ENG editors are expected to be able to maintain and repair their own equipment as many of them work away from base.

Film Editor (see p 39)

Electrician
Production electricians, also known as lighting electricians, follow the plans of the lighting director and arrange lamps in a way that will produce the desired lighting effects. They may work in a studio, on location or take part in outside broadcasts. They repair and maintain the apparatus they use.

Engineer

Engineers, technical assistants and technical operators have a vital role to play in broadcasting, but it is beyond the scope of this book to describe all the jobs available in this large field. Such information can be obtained from the training adviser of the Independent Television Companies Association and from the Engineering Recruitment Office of the BBC. A few successful graduates in electronics, electrical engineering and applied physics are recruited for direct appointment as engineers.

Operational engineers are responsible for the technical facilities needed for the production and transmission of radio and television programmes. They may be involved in studio work, outside broadcasts, the operation and maintenance of the networks, recording, news-gathering and transmission systems (eg cable and satellite) etc. Some work at base and spend their days sitting at a control desk. Others are out with mobile recording units, at transmitter sites, on location or on overseas assignments.

Specialist engineers work in research departments developing new techniques and systems and improving existing equipment, in design departments and in capital projects departments.

Technical assistants, when training to become engineers, provide the support force for qualified engineers. They set up, align and maintain broadcasting equipment and in some cases operate it.

Technical operators are the junior members of a skilled team and they help with the preparation and operation of equipment.

Floor Manager

Floor managers, who have an important and demanding job, are rarely recruited externally; as a rule, they start their careers as assistants. They need to be thoroughly familiar with every aspect of television production. One part of their work is to provide the link between the programme director and the studio floor. During studio rehearsals and recordings the programme director normally watches proceedings on television monitors and can speak to the floor manager through the talkback system. It is the floor manager who passes on the director's instructions to performers and also gives cues and prompts.

Floor managers co-ordinate and manage everything that happens on the studio floor, making sure that performers know where to stand and what to do, that props are in place and microphones and cameras are correctly positioned etc. They are in charge of a studio audience when there is one.

BROADCASTING

Graphic Designer and **Graphic Design Assistant** (see p 137)

Journalism and News Work (see p 73)

Legal Work (see p 169)

Librarian (see p 161)

Lighting Director
Lighting directors decide how to position lights on a set in order to produce the best effect. In a chat show, for example, this would be relatively simple, but in a play lighting is used to create atmosphere and illusion. Lighting directors liaise with set designers, make-up artists and other members of the production team and prepare plans for the lighting electricians and lighting console operators, whose work they supervise. (See also **Lighting Cameraman/woman**, p 38.)

Lighting Electrician (see **Electrician**, p 19)

Make-up Artist (see p 52)

Marketing Staff
Any broadcasting company that tries to make money from the sale of its programmes employs marketing staff who need a detailed knowledge not only of company output but also of potential foreign markets. (See Chapter 11.)

Model Maker (see **Visual Effects Designer** p 27)

Music Presenter
This is one of the most sought-after jobs in radio. The position carries considerable responsibility as the DJ is, more often than not, the station's image-figure. A music presenter has to be a very good all-rounder; in addition to technical experience (music presenters in local radio handle their own studio equipment), the job calls for a wide general background including a grasp of current affairs, an easy microphone manner, a pleasant voice and the ability to think quickly and to ad lib. The work includes a lot of routine tasks, eg listing running orders, timing programmes and logging records for royalty payments.

CAREERS IN THE MEDIA

News Work

News readers, also called news presenters, newscasters and anchormen/women, are frequently experienced journalists (see Chapter 5). They present the news from the studio, reading some items themselves and linking and introducing stories from reporters. They may read from a script that has been prepared by someone else or one they have written themselves. They must be thoroughly acquainted with the background to the news and must check such things as the pronunciation of foreign names. They must be able to read at sight without fluffing, as stories may break in the middle of a bulletin, and to vary the pace of their delivery in order to fit in with time signals and call signs.

News typists have the important and demanding task of typing news bulletins; they must be able to take dictation directly on to the typewriter and do audio and copy typing.

Performer (see Chapter 4)

Personnel Work (see p 169)

Plumber (see p 51)

Presenter

Presenters 'front' (or host) current affairs programmes, quizzes, games and chat shows etc and they are usually well-known public personalities in such fields as sport, journalism or the theatre. Presenters' jobs are not advertised; presenters are normally approached and offered a contract for a programme or series.

Producer

Many people confuse the roles of producer and director. In some productions the same person takes on both roles, but when the jobs are separated it is the producer who heads the production team and who will probably have originated, or contributed to, the idea on which the programme is based. In addition, the producer manages the programme budget and the scheduling of rehearsals and recording/shooting and has a say in the selection of actors/participants and members of the production team. Every programme has a producer and most producers specialise. For example, a radio talk on current affairs needs a producer with a good grasp of the subject and sound political judgement; a television wildlife programme might need a producer with the organisational skill and experience to get a large production team and expensive equipment to the Sahara. Most vacancies are filled by internal applicants. There are a few traineeships for graduates.

Production Assistant

Production assistants work on a particular programme from start to finish, providing support for the programme director. They attend all programme planning meetings, take notes of the decisions made and see that the required action is taken. If during rehearsal the programme director decides to change the script, the production assistant notes the changes and retypes the script. Many production assistants do the work of the continuity person (see p 37). In the final run-through of a television production, the production assistant sits with the programme director in the control room and instructs the camera operators over the talkback system, and in both radio and television productions the production assistant times recordings or takes with a stopwatch. The production assistant will provide any information needed by those engaged on post-production work.

Production assistants also work on live programmes, eg news, concerts, sporting events, and the atmosphere in the control room during transmission can be very tense. The work calls for excellent organisational skills, attention to detail, calm, initiative and the ability to manage and get on with all types of people.

Most production assistants are recruited as trainees and many vacancies for traineeships are filled by people already in broadcasting.

Programme Director

The programme director in television is in charge of the shooting of a programme and the direction of performers and technical crews. When the shooting is over, the director supervises post-production work such as editing and sound dubbing. In a live broadcast, eg a news bulletin, the programme director follows a running order, selects pictures from those offered by the camera operator or from videotape and relays instructions to the presenters.

In radio drama the director rehearses the actors, selects sound effects and, after recording, supervises the post-production work of editing and dubbing.

Most vacancies are filled by internal applicants with substantial experience.

Projectionist (Film Assistant) (see p 39)

CAREERS IN THE MEDIA

Property Staff (see p 52)

Public Relations Officer (see Chapter 10)

Publishing Work (see Chapter 6)

Reporter (see p 71)

Researcher
Behind nearly every successful programme there will have been a hard-working, competent researcher, who has sought out the practical elements of, say, a story and put them into a form which can be incorporated in the programme. News, news magazine and current affairs programmes require extensive collaboration from researchers who are expected to contribute ideas for the programme and prepare material for particular items. Researchers find suitable people for interviews and write script treatments for the programme presenter; they may have to trace pictures in newspaper archives, sequences in old newsreels or recordings from sound archives. General research tasks could include looking up bibliographical details for a book programme, testing consumer reactions to a new product for a food programme or finding participants for a quiz or panel game. A few researchers are permanent employees of broadcasting organisations, but most of them are freelances who are hired on contract to work on a particular film, radio or television programme or series. (See also **Picture Research**, p 86.)

Rostrum Camera Operator (see p 138)

Sales Staff (independent/commercial sector only)
Those radio and television companies whose revenue comes from the sale of advertising time employ sales staff – *sales co-ordinators* negotiate the sale of airtime, take bookings and see that 'slots' are filled; *sales or marketing executives* are responsible for attracting new business; *sales research staff* carry out and interpret market research; *traffic staff* monitor the make-up of commercial breaks and arrange for the receipt and delivery of advertisements. (See also Chapter 11.)

Scenic Artist and Painter (see p 51)

BROADCASTING

Script Editor

Script editors work in drama departments. One of their tasks may be to act as intermediary between the writer and producer and some script editors commission new work. The original idea for a serial usually comes from one person, but a number of writers will be needed to produce episodes in a uniform style, sometimes over many years, following a storyline which the script editor may have prepared. Script editors generally have a literary background and have worked in the theatre, reading and reporting on unsolicited scripts.

Script Girl (see **Continuity**, p 37)

Secretary and Clerk (see p 170)

Set Designer (see p 48)

Setting Assistant (see **Stagehand**, below)

Sound Operator

Sound operators are employed in both radio and television and their work requires technical skill and creativity. In a radio studio duties include: sound balancing and mixing, tape recording, disc playing and selecting sound effects. In a television studio *sound technicians* see that studio equipment is working properly and that microphone and boom arms are positioned so as to remain out of camera shot. They work closely with the camera operators. There is a sound control room where technicians monitor the sound signals and feed music or other sound effects into the programme and balance the sound. All sound technicians do a lot of pre- and post-production work. They edit taped speech and music and select, or in some cases devise, special sound effects.

Sound technicians work on outside broadcasts, eg matches and state occasions. In the outside broadcast unit, which is a large vehicle equipped like a sound studio, sound signals are mixed and monitored. Staff are responsible for rigging up equipment and testing the quality of lines.

Stagehand

Stagehands, also known as setting assistants, usually work in small teams. They erect the scenery in a studio or on location and dismantle it when shooting or transmission is finished. Most television scenery consists of large plywood flats which must be assembled according to the designer's plans. The work is strenuous. Trainee stagehands should be aged between 18 and 45 and be physically fit. They need no special educational qualifications, though GCSEs (or equivalents) in English, mathematics and technical drawing would be useful, as would a clean driving licence.

Stage Manager
Stage managers organise outside rehearsals, which usually take place in large public halls, order and move props and note any changes made to the script during rehearsals. They also mark out the rehearsal room floor and prompt. Only people with experience are recruited. (See also p 49.)

Studio Manager
Studio managers have an important and demanding job that calls for creative flair, technical competence, organising ability and a cool head. They have to see that the radio producer's/director's instructions are carried out and this involves setting up the studio for recording or transmission, checking equipment, adjusting sound balance controls, monitoring sound quality, running tapes and discs at the right moment and co-ordinating the activities of the people participating in the programme, who might be actors, musicians, a studio audience, people called for interview etc. Studio managers usually start as trainees and then specialise in, for example, music broadcasts, current affairs or drama.

Technical Assistant/Operator (see **Engineer**, p 20)

Television Recording Operator
Television recording operators control film and telecine equipment and videotape machines. They must understand the capabilities of the equipment and appreciate the artistic requirements of the production on which they are involved.

Television Set Designer (see p 138)

Transmission Controller
Transmission controllers send the broadcasting organisation's programme output to the transmitters. This output might originate in a number of different places and it is sent via land line or other links to local transmitters. Transmission controllers sit at a presentation mixer console on which they can monitor the picture that is going from point

or origin to transmitter, the picture going from transmitter to home television screen and the opening sequence from the next programme, and they press the controls to bring in each programme on cue. The work involves a great deal of planning and combines periods of intense activity with periods during which nothing much happens.

Vision Mixer
A television programme may be made up of pictures that come from a number of different sources, eg from a camera in the studio, from pre-recorded videotape, from a telecine machine or from a slide. Vision mixers receive a signal from the director telling them when to cut from one picture source to another producing a smooth sequence of images. The vision mixer sits at a console into which all the picture sources are fed; This console can produce special effects, eg dissolving or wiping, to make the transition from one scene to another either interesting or unobtrusive. The job calls for quick reactions and an excellent sense of timing.

Visual Effects Designer
Visual effects designers construct and carry out all sorts of visual effects, such as a 'Fire of London' or a rocket launch. They use scale models, made by model makers from a variety of materials such as wood, plastic, papier mâché or fibreglass. Visual effects staff need a good working knowledge of sculpture, model making, painting, optics, pyrotechnics, together with an understanding of the principles of physics, chemistry and electricity.

Wardrobe Work (see p 52)

Writer (see Chapter 8)

The Employers

The BBC
By far the biggest employer among the broadcasting organisations is the BBC which, with its domestic and external services, is concerned with all aspects of broadcasting. These include news gathering, programme making, selling programmes to foreign buyers, audience reseach and the development, running and maintenance of the transmitter networks. There are two television channels, BBC1 and BBC2, Radios 1, 2, 3 and

4, 31 local radio stations, the External Services, the World Service, the Monitoring Service, Ceefax and a number of commercial activities. The Corporation employs in all some 28,000 people and much of its outside recruitment is at assistant level for it has its own competitive promotion and transfer system, an integral part of which is the attachment scheme. Employees who have applied for promotion or transfer and who have shown particular aptitude and commitment are given the opportunity to work in a new post for a trial period of six months. When this period is up, the employees on attachment compete with other applicants for the post; if they turn out not to be of the calibre the post demands they can return to their old post which will have been kept open.

The Independent Sector
Over 20,000 people work in independent broadcasting and this figure can be roughly broken down as follows: 15,000 are employed by the independent television area contractors, TV-am, Independent Television News (ITN), ORACLE and Channel Four Television Company; some 2000 work in independent local radio (ILR) and 1500 in the Independent Broadcasting Authority. There are also large numbers of people associated with independent broadcasting who work in independent production companies (see p 30) and ancillary organisations.

The IBA fulfils the wishes of Parliament in providing television and radio services of information, education and entertainment additional to those of the BBC. It also ensures that they are of a high standard. Its four main functions are: to select and appoint the ITV and ILR companies, supervise the programming, control the advertising and transmit the output.

The Independent Television Area Contractors
There are 15 totally separate regional television companies each with its own operating, recruiting and training policies. These are Anglia Television, Border Television, Central Independent Television, HTV (Wales and West of England), London Weekend Television, Scottish Television, Thames Television, TSW (Television South West), Television South, Tyne Tees Television, Ulster Television and Yorkshire Television. These companies vary considerably in size and employment profiles; all provide programmes for the network and make regional programmes for their area audience.

Channel Four Television Company Ltd
Channel Four Television Company Ltd provides a national service

networked to the whole of the UK except Wales. It offers a more limited range of jobs than the other independent television companies because it does not make programmes or sell advertising time.

Sianel Pedwar Cymru (S4C)
Sianel Pedwar Cymru (S4C), the Welsh Fourth Channel Authority, schedules some 22 hours of Welsh language programmes supplied by outside bodies. In addition, it relays most of Channel Four's 70 hours of programmes.

TV-am
TV-am, which holds the franchise for breakfast-time television, is a wholly independent company selling its own advertising time and originating its own output.

Independent Television News (ITN)
ITN is a London-based company owned by all 15 regional television companies, whose main function is to provide the daily programmes of national and international news for the independent television network and a weekday news and news analysis programme for Channel Four.

Independent Local Radio (ILR)
There are 48 ILR stations around the country, each an independent company and each with its own strongly local character. The London Broadcasting Company (LBC) is different from other ILR stations as it is solely a news and information station. Independent Radio News (IRN) is its wholly owned subsidiary.

Radio Luxembourg (London) Ltd
Radio Luxembourg is a company wholly owned by Radio Tele Luxembourge (RTL); it is responsible for operating the English Service on 208m and Community Service (local FM programme in Luxembourg) and represents RTL's interests in the UK.

Manx Radio
Manx Radio operates on a licence issued by the British Post Office under UK wireless telegraphy legislation, but the programme content is entirely the prerogative of the Isle of Man authorities.

CAREERS IN THE MEDIA

The Services Sound and Vision Corporation (SSVC) and the British Forces Broadcasting Service (BFBS)
The SSVC provides the Armed Forces with a variety of entertainment, engineering support and training services; its output consists almost entirely of programmes taken from the BBC and IBA channels under contract. BFBS London does not transmit live but records some 50 hours of speech and music every week.

Cable Television
Cable television is slowly spreading throughout the country and there are now over 20 cable television companies in existence. Their names and addresses can be obtained from the Cable Authority, Gillingham House, 38-44 Gillingham Street, London SW1V 1HU. There are also several companies known as programme providers whose programmes are beamed by satellite to cable headends and then carried on cable systems.

Satellite Broadcasting
At present there are two satellite broadcasting companies in the UK, the British Satellite Broadcasting consortium (BSB) and Rupert Murdoch's Sky Television. Both plan to go on the air in 1989.

Radio
The government is planning to set up a radio authority in the summer of 1989. Once this has been established, national commercial radio services will be introduced and, as new frequencies become available, several hundred community radio stations will be given permission to go on the air.

Independent Television Production Companies
There are a great many independent television production companies making anything from full-length television programmes for transmission on the national networks to commercials, publicity, educational and training material. Some of these companies employ a full complement of technical and production personnel; some are run by a skeleton staff and hire freelance directors and crews for specific assignments. Independent production companies are listed in Kemps' *International Film and Television Yearbook* and *The Electronic Media Directory and New Media Yearbook* published by WOAC Communications Company. (See also Chapter 2.)

Job Prospects

New broadcasting companies are being set up and new jobs being created all the time, but the competition for posts remains extremely tough. Many people are so keen to get into broadcasting that they put in for posts they would not dream of accepting in any other sector, in the hope that once inside they will be able to work their way up. The only area which is short of applicants is engineering.

What people do not always realise is that a great many broadcasters do not have permanent salaried status but are freelances with a contract for a single programme or series of programmes. This is true not only of the best-known personalities in broadcasting, the show hosts, quiz chairmen and actors – many of whom do a lot of work outside radio and television – but of other categories of employee.

Many people begin a career in broadcasting in local radio; there are BBC and independent local stations all over the UK and in a few years' time there will be a network of community stations. There is a lot of inter-media mobility: staff move from local to national radio, from radio to television, back and forth between the theatre, films and television and from newspaper journalism to radio or television journalism. There is no such thing as a typical career path in broadcasting and promotion is on merit.

Getting Started

Intense competition makes it very difficult to get started on a broadcasting career and one thing that will give you the edge over other applicants for a post is relevant work experience. If you want to work in news, current affairs or documentaries experience in journalism or film making is what you need. For drama and light entertainment, theatrical knowledge and backstage experience are useful. Hospital or campus radio experience is also useful; you can learn to handle broadcasting equipment, develop microphone techniques and you discover how hard it is to fill airtime with good, original material.

Many people feel that local radio is more approachable than national and station managers are always on the look-out for new talent of all kinds; they are also permanently in need of material and are glad to be put on the track of local news, sports news, news from schools and colleges, people to interview and places to visit. Local radio is indeed *local* and whenever possible employs people with local ties and local knowledge. It is sometimes possible to get a foot in the door by doing voluntary, temporary or part-time work. Station managers receive a great many unsolicited demo tapes and a good rule to observe when making a demo tape is *keep it short*. An all-rounder's tape might contain a two-minute news reading (this would be a piece of about 250 words), a well-structured interview lasting about three minutes and a sample of how you introduce music. *In all 10 minutes maximum.* Job advertisements appear in the quality press and the *Listener*.

Personal Qualities

Broadcasting is full of bright, ambitious and committed people who are able to perform well under pressure. Whatever the post you apply for, your interviewers will want to be sure that you are capable of working in a team, as radio and television work is team work. To take a somewhat extreme example, a television play involves scores of people: the cast, the make-up and wardrobe teams, lighting, sound and camera crews, scene and prop hands, the stage manager, floor manager, production assistant and producer. These are only the people you will find in the studio. Before the production can get to the studio, writers, musicians, legal experts, accountants, scene designers and secretaries will have been involved, and when shooting is over there is work for editors and dubbing mixers. All these people have to work together to get the play on to the screen on time.

Salaries

It is difficult to give any meaningful information on salaries; they vary from one company to another, change regularly and many salaried staff receive considerably more than their basic pay each month because of overtime, regional weightings and shift allowances etc.

Equal Opportunities

The broadcasting organisations are in theory equal opportunities employers, but in practice there are few women and members of ethnic minorities in the top jobs. There are some signs of change; for example, the BBC is currently running a course to train six Asians and Afro-Caribbeans as reporters and presenters. (See also p 22 and 71)

Union Membership (see p 41)

Entry Requirements and Training

Job titles, job descriptions and entry requirements vary from one broadcasting organisation to another. Certain traineeships require applicants to have some professional and/or academic qualifications; others require none. People who apply for a first job in radio or television, particularly if it is a traineeship, are usually in their early twenties. There are openings for school-leavers in craft, clerical or junior posts and on apprenticeship schemes. Qualified personnel are generally recruited to fill administrative posts. Certain posts, like that of producer or floor manager, are open only to internal applicants.

A number of institutions offer courses on broadcasting-related subjects; however, the broadcasting organisations, while acknowledging that many of the courses are of a good standard, do not officially recognise them. The organisations which recruit trainees put them through a house training scheme.

Courses and Awards

CNAA BA Hons Applied photography, film and television, Harrow CHE
CNAA BA Hons Photography, film and video, animation, West Surrey CAD
CNAA BA Hons Drama, theatre and television studies, King Alfred's C, Winchester
CNAA Diploma Film and television studies, Sunderland Poly
BA Hons Visual and performed arts, film studies, U of Kent
Diploma in television and video, London Goldsmiths' C
Combined subjects degree: Radio, film and television studies option, Canterbury Christ Church
Combined subjects degree: Drama, film and television option, Ripon and York, St John C

BTEC HND Film and television specialism, Bournemouth and Poole
CAD, Gwent CHE
College award: Diploma in drama and television studies, Southampton TC
College-based course: Television, film and visual communication techniques, Chippenham TC
See also Chapters 2 and 3.

Further Information

BBC Annual Report and Handbook
Careers in Independent Television (Independent Television Companies Association)
Careers in Television and Radio (Kogan Page)
Television and Radio (IBA yearbook)

Broadcast
Keen to Be in Television? and *Behind the Scenes in Television* (Royal Television Society)
Stage and Television Today
Televisual

Always send a self-addressed stamped envelope.
Association of Cinematograph, Television and Allied Technicians (ACTT), 111 Wardour Street, London W1V 4AY
BBC Appointments Department, Broadcasting House, London W1A 1AA
Independent Broadcasting Authority, 70 Brompton Road, London SW3 1EY
Independent Television Companies Association, Training Adviser, Knighton House, 56 Mortimer Street, London W1N 8AN
The Royal Television Society, Tavistock House East, Tavistock Square, London WC1H 9HR
(See also p 45.)

Chapter 2
Film and Video Industries

Film and videotape are both used to record moving images. The images recorded on film are of a higher quality and are, therefore, more suitable for projection on a cinema screen. Film cameras allow directors more creative scope than video cameras and many television commercials are produced on film. Video equipment is cheaper and easier to use. Much of it is light and electronic news-gathering (ENG) equipment can be used by one person, making it ideal for news reporting.

The film and video industries also, of course, provide work for actors (p 55), agents (p 157), graphic artists/designers (pp 131, 137), hairdressers (p 52), make-up artists (p 52), set designers (p 139), and wardrobe and property staff (p 52).

The Film Industry

The British film industry, located mainly in and around London, consists for the most part of production companies, studios, post-production houses and film distributors. This chapter also contains a short section on the work of cinema staff.

Production companies, of which there are large numbers, make the films. They tend to keep their permanent staff to a minimum – perhaps just one or more producers and directors, a secretary or personal assistant, a receptionist and a runner (also called a messenger or gofer) – and hire freelance technical staff for each production. Their output is varied, including feature films, which are specifically intended for cinema release, though they will be shown on television after a certain number of years; television programmes (documentaries and shorts) and television commercials; other advertising and PR material; scientific, educational and training films.

Studios, such as Pinewood and Elstree, which used to make films, now let space and facilities to production companies which bring their own crews with them.

The post-production sector of the industry includes the film laboratories and companies providing facilities like editing rooms, sound recording studios, and such services as opticals and special effects.

Film distributors handle the marketing and publicity for films as well as co-ordinating the physical distribution of film prints to cinemas and screening rooms. Most of the jobs are clerical.

There are three stages in film-making: pre-production, production and post-production. The first stage involves the producer, who has the initial idea and must then obtain financial backing to realise it. He/she hires the director and has a hand in casting, finding locations and hiring the crew. Production, the shooting of the film, is done on location or in a studio. The director, the cast (possibly including extras and stunt performers – (see p 63), the assistant director, the camera, lighting and sound personnel, stage crew, dressers, hairdressers and make-up artists are all actively involved. The post-production stage, which may take longer than the shooting, is the processing and editing.

The Video Industry

This rapidly expanding sector is not as London-centred as the film industry. It makes features and commercials for transmission on television and a great deal of non-broadcast material, eg training, point-of-sale and promotional videos. The set-up is like that of the film industry; there are small production companies consisting of perhaps four full-time employees and an *ad hoc* team is assembled for each production.

The Jobs

Whether you are producing a three-minute training video or a three-hour screen epic, the same basic process is involved. The work of all the people mentioned below has to be done, though in the case of the video production several people's work may be done by just one person.

Producer
It is the producer who controls the organisation and budget and puts the entire package together. He/she usually comes up with the idea for the film, obtains the rights to the property if, for example, it is a book or oversees the writing of an original screenplay, and is responsible for raising the money. When production begins, the producer monitors its

day-to-day progress and sees to it that the film will be completed on time and to the agreed budget.

In the case of a video production there is generally a client, eg a bank or large department store, and the producer puts forward outline proposals, including a cost breakdown, for the client's approval and then assembles a production team.

Good producers are interested in a wide range of subjects and are always coming up with new ideas for productions. They need to be very determined and persuasive and to possess business acumen and organising skills. Producing is seldom a first job; many producers started out in business or were agents, production managers, or assistant directors.

Director
Directors have to decide how best to use the technical and artistic resources. They direct both actors and the camera and for this reason must understand such things as lenses, lights, editing processes and acting techniques and they need a strong visual sense. They are in complete charge of the studio or location floor and have the last word on all creative matters. Directors have often gained experience working in television or learning a specialist skill and many young directors have taken a film-school course.

Casting Director (see p 47)

Continuity
The person in charge of continuity is often called the 'script girl'; there are a lot of women in continuity work, possibly because it requires a highly developed sense of observation and great attention to detail. It is the continuity person's job to ensure that the film/video looks as if it were all shot without a break. He/she sees to it that everything, from the position of props, arrangement of clothing, gestures and voice inflections, matches from shot to shot. The work involves keeping detailed notes of each shot and a log of each day's work.

Production Manager
The production manager is, in effect, the producer's deputy and is actively involved in the day-to-day problems of filming. It is the production manager's job to prepare a detailed budget for shooting and a shooting schedule, to hire equipment and, when necessary, obtain permission to film in certain locations. In a large-scale production there may be a line producer, who is in charge of administrative questions such

as budgeting, crew hire and contracts, and a location manager, who finds locations, obtains permission to use them, and is responsible for seeing that they are left in good condition when shooting is over.

Assistant Director

There are usually three assistant directors and, despite their name, the second and third work more closely with the production department than with the director. The first assistant does help the director but acts as deputy only in crowd scenes. He/she anticipates the director's practical requirements, supervises the discipline and general organisation of the daily shooting schedule, prepares call sheets and checks with the production manager that the technical needs for the next day's shooting will be met. Most first assistant directors go on to become producers.

The second and third assistant directors will have been chosen by the first as people he/she can work with. The second assistant prepares for the following day's or week's shooting, making sure that the cast and equipment needed will be ready. The third assistant works on the set, sees that the actors receive their call, keeps the production running smoothly and acts as the legs of the first assistant.

The assistant directors as a team are responsible for keeping a good atmosphere on the set and it can be their job to let the director know when the crew or actors are tired or dissatisfied. They are there to maximise efficiency and anticipate problems.

Lighting Cameraman/woman

The lighting cameraman/woman (also called cinematographer or director of photography) is, after the director, the most creative member of the team. He/she works very closely with the director, deciding how each shot should look, lighting it and choosing camera angles, lenses, filters, but not positioning or handling the camera. This is one of the most sought-after posts in the industry; film-school training or an apprenticeship can both be ways in. There are very few camerawomen.

Camera Operator

Camera operator and lighting cameraman/woman often form themselves into a team and go together from production to production. The camera operator attends to the physical details of each shot. He/she generally has three assistants: the *focus puller*, who measures the distance between camera and subject and needs to possess considerable technical

FILM AND VIDEO INDUSTRIES

knowledge; the *clapper/loader*, who loads the cameras, logs each shot and operates the clapper board before each shot; the *camera grip*, who moves the camera dolly and manoeuvres it during tracking shots.

Sound personnel

The *sound mixer* records the sound on location and balances sound levels. The *sound recordist* is the sound mixer's assistant.

The *boom handler* controls the microphones which are hung out of camera shot; their position is determined by the mixer or recordist.

The *dubbing mixer* works on the post-production phase of the film, supervising the recording of additional sound, including music and special effects, deciding on the appropriate level of sound and matching image to sound (post-synching). The dubbing mixer's job is both technical and creative and it takes years of experience to become qualified.

Editor

Though most of an editor's work takes place during the post-production phase, some minor editing goes on during shooting. It is the editor who determines the narrative structure of the film by cutting and assembling it. The basics of cutting are not difficult to learn, but it is very hard to progress from cutting to the creative task of editing. The editor usually has two assistants, who collect the rushes, put location sound to picture for viewing and join the cuts under the editor's supervision. Experience can be gained by editing students' films.

Projectionist (Film Assistant)

Projectionists operate projection equipment in dubbing and viewing studios and may be involved in dubbing work, eg combining a number of sound tracks, perhaps those containing music or special effects, to produce the final sound track.

Other jobs include subtitling and dubbing (providing spoken dialogue in a language other than that in which the film has been recorded).

There are also jobs in cinemas. There are two large firms owning chains of cinemas and a number of independent houses. Nowadays, the big city cinemas tend to have several auditoria and employ a general manager, a house or theatre manager (see p 50), a box office manager (see p 50), attendants (ushers/usherettes), and sales staff. A small independent cinema will probably be staffed by volunteer workers or part-timers and have very few full-time salaried employees.

General managers who work for a chain will probably have most of their programming handled by head office, but they should have the opportunity to plan special morning or late-night programmes. The general managers of independent cinemas are free to do their own programming; they keep themselves informed by reading press releases and reviews and attending previews and film festivals. The other duties include handling publicity and hiring out the premises for such things as concerts or public meetings.

Getting Started (Film Industry)

It is very difficult to get started on a career in films, not simply because of the strong competition for jobs, but because the trade unions operate a closed shop. Unless you have successfully completed a course at one of the schools recognised by the unions, the first job you apply for will have to be one that does not require union membership; for example, runner, secretary or receptionist. Production and post-production companies usually have one or two runners on their staff and they also hire runners for a specific production.

Being a *runner* is an excellent way to begin a career. Many film companies, without offering formal training, will give you the opportunity to learn as much as you want; if you join an equipment-hire company you will be able to learn the technical side of film-making. Jobs usually go to young people, aged 16 or 17, who live in or around London. You may need a driving licence and, because the pay is low, it is easier to manage if you are living with your parents. Jobs are rarely advertised so you must write to, or telephone, companies or go in person to ask about jobs. If you perform well as a runner, you can expect promotion but this rarely comes quickly. After 300 shooting days you become eligible for ACTT membership.

Secretaries or receptionists can move into production work. Most companies hire people aged at least 18 who have good office skills.

Film-processing laboratories generally have permanent staff only and there are few posts for beginners. A vacancy in a laboratory must be notified to the union and only if there is no qualified union member available to fill it can it be advertised externally.

Getting Started (Video Industry)

Video cameras are relatively cheap and easy to use and one way to get started in the industry is to set yourself up as a one-person production company offering a recording service for weddings and other social events.

There is a growing market for this kind of service now that so many people own videotape recorders. Orders and other types of assignment will start to come your way as your work becomes known.

Equal Opportunities

There are few women and even fewer members of ethnic minorities represented in the film and video industries. But things are beginning to change; some film schools are actively encouraging women and members of ethnic minorities to apply for places, there have been cases of government funds being withheld until certain staffing quotas were met, one or two training schemes for members of ethnic minorities have been set up, and the new equipment is much lighter and therefore easier for women to handle.

Union Membership

The Association of Cinematograph, Television and Allied Technicians (ACTT) is the main union for most technical/production jobs in the industry. It covers a wide range of occupations and a highly fragmented industry throughout the UK and procedures vary from sector to sector. In order to obtain ACTT membership you need to be offered an ACTT-graded job which has been advertised through the Union's employment bureau and to complete an application form. Your application is then considered by the appropriate local group of members who will recommend a decision to the Union's executive body. Because the Union covers such a great variety of sectors, you should contact the ACTT's employment and membership officer who will be able to give you relevant and up-to-date information.

CAREERS IN THE MEDIA

Entry Requirements and Training

It has always been, and still is, possible to start at the very bottom of the ladder in the film industry with few or no academic qualifications and work your way to the top. This can be a very slow process, but there are those who believe that it is the best thing to do because of the invaluable experience you accumulate on the way.

There are seven institutions which run ACTT-accredited film and television courses. Students who successfully complete one of these courses are entitled to full unrestricted union membership upon finding ACTT-graded work. The institutions are: The National Film and Television School, Beaconsfield; the West Surrey College of Art and Design, Farnham; The Polytechnic of Central London; The London International Film School; Bristol University's Film and Television Department, The London College of Printing; Bournemouth and Poole College of Art and Design.

Recently there has been an enormous expansion of training opportunities in film, video and sound. According to the ACTT, 'they range from the worthwhile, thorough and "free" to the appalling and expensive' and you are strongly recommended to make careful enquiries before paying course fees. A number of schemes set up by the ACTT and employers within the industry offer a combination of industry placements and college-based off-the-job training. The following are the ones with which the Union has had most dealings and which have positive action policies on equality:

Joint Board for Film Industry Training (JOBFIT), 5 Dean Street, London W1V 5RN. A two-year scheme for people aged 18+ who want to work as freelance technicians in the film industry.
Opportunity (Cyfle), Gronant, Penrallt Isaf, Caernarfon, Gwynedd LL55 1NW. A two-year scheme training Welsh-speaking technicians for the film and television industry in Wales.
North-East Media Training Centre (NEMTC), Stonehills, Shields Road, Gateshead, Tyne and Wear NE10 0HW. A two-year scheme training people who want to work as technicians and production workers in the workshops and collectives of the north east.
Scottish Film Training Trust (SFTT), Dowanhill, 74 Victoria Crescent Road, Glasgow G12 9JN. A one-year scheme training technicians for the Scottish film and television industry.

Competition for every training place is tough and you should apply as

FILM AND VIDEO INDUSTRIES

early as possible. If you are asked to attend an interview you will be expected to show samples of your work, eg a short film or a script. It is not enough simply to be 'interested'; you will be expected to have had some practical experience or involvement. Many people have audiotape equipment and hundreds of schools, community centres and employment projects have video/film-making equipment which you should try to use (for example, take a local authority evening course). Throughout the country there are short courses run by collectives/workshops; you can find out about these from the BFI's training co-ordinator. Though these courses are not accepted as vocational/professional training, they offer the opportunity to gain the experience you will need in order to be accepted for a recognised course.

Other Courses and Awards

University First Degrees
MA Ord/Hons and MA (Soc Sci) Ord/Hons Film and television studies, Glasgow
BA Education/music with radio, film and television studies, Kent
Combined subjects degree: Radio, film and television studies option, Kent
BA Hons Film studies, Kent
BSc and BA General film and media studies, Stirling
BA Hons Film and literature, Warwick

Polytechnic CNAA Degrees
BA Hons Film and photographic arts, Central London
BA/BA Hons Film, video and photographic arts, Central London
BA Hons Design for communication media (film and television), Manchester
BA Hons modular scheme History of art, design and film, Middlesex
BA/BA Hons Design and film, Newcastle upon Tyne
BA Hons English – Film studies, North London
BA Hons History of Design and the Visual Arts, North Staffordshire
BA/BA Hons History of art, design and film, Sheffield

Higher Degrees awarded by Universities
MA Film studies, East Anglia
MA Theatre and media production, Hull
MA, MSc, LLM, MPhil, Film studies, Kent

CAREERS IN THE MEDIA

MA Film and television studies for education, London I of Education;
MA (RCA) Animation; Photography; Film design for the moving image; Film making; Film productions; Graphics in film and television, Royal CA
MA The periodical press in Britain 1580-1914, Wales

Diplomas awarded by universities
Diploma, Television and Video; Theatre skills, U London, Goldsmiths' C

Diplomas awarded by Polytechnics
BTEC HND Photographic technology, Manchester
Postgraduate CNAA Diploma, Video, Middlesex

Certificates awarded by Universities
U of London Certificate Holography as art, Goldsmiths' C
Extra-mural Certificate and Diploma Film studies, London Extra-Mural Studies Department

Certificates awarded by Polytechnics
Polytechnic Certificate Printing and photographic technology, Manchester

College-based Courses and Degrees
CNAA BA Hons Applied photography, film and television, Harrow CHE
CNAA BA Hons Visual communications (film and video), London C of Printing
CNAA BA Hons Photography, film and video animation, West Surrey CA&D
Combined subjects degree: Film and drama option, Bulmershe CHE
Combined subjects degree: Drama, film and television option, Ripon and York, St John C
Combined studies degree: Modern English studies, film and literature option, West Glamorgan IHE
BTEC HND Film and television specialism, Bournemouth and Poole CA&D, Gwent CHE
City and Guilds 6996 Foundation course in multimedia communications technology, Watford C
College award: Certificate in film studies, Havering TC
Course in film and drama studies, Chichester CT

FILM AND VIDEO INDUSTRIES

Course in television, film and visual communication techniques, Chippenham TC

Professional Body

The British Kinematograph Sound and Television Society Ltd, 547-549 Victoria House, Vernon Place, London WC1B 4DJ has four categories of membership: Fellow, Corporate member, Associate member, Student member.

Further Information

Always send a self-addressed stamped envelope.

Association of Cinematograph, Television and Allied Technicians (ACTT), 111 Wardour Street, London W1V 4AY
The British Film Institute (Education Department), 21 Stephen Street, London W1P 1PL
The BFI Film Society Unit, 21 Stephen Street, London W1P 1PL
The Independent Film, Video and Photography Association, 79 Wardour Street, London W1V 3PH
Scottish Film Council, Dowanhill, 74 Victoria Crescent Road, Glasgow G12 9JN
Society for Education in Film and Television, 29 Old Compton Street, London W1V 5PL
The Women's Film Television and Video Network, 79 Wardour Street, London W1V 3PH

Careers in Film and Video (Kogan Page)
Careers in Film and Television and *Film Schools* (British Film Institute)
Film and Television Training (British Film Institute)
Education and Training for Film and Television (British Kinematograph Sound and Television Society)
A Woman's Guide to Jobs in Film and Television (Pandora Press)
Working in Television and Video (COIC)

Chapter 3
Theatre

This chapter is about careers in the theatre but does not include acting, which is covered in Chapter 4 p 55-63. The different kinds of theatre (subsidised, commercial, repertory etc) are described in Chapter 4, pp 56-7. Many of the jobs outlined in this chapter could also be done in a ballet company, an opera house, in television or in films and, one or two of them, in a concert hall or arts centre. There is a separate chapter (Chapter 15) on arts administration, and information about theatrical agency work on pp 157-8 of Chapter 16.

You can get some idea of the range and variety of jobs in a theatre by looking at the small print in a theatre programme. At the top of the scale of employers are the National Theatre of Great Britain, which has three theatres under one roof and employs 550 full-time staff (including cleaners and catering staff but excluding actors), and the Royal Shakespeare Company, which runs five theatres and is the biggest theatre company in the world.

An RSC programme has a formidable list of credits: two joint artistic directors, technical administrator, general manager, controller, financial controller, departments covering voice, technical systems, scenic art, sponsorship, wigs, make-up, merchandising, casting, construction, wardrobe, safety, music, publicity, scenic workshop, property shop and paint shop, company manager, chief lighting operator, chief lighting engineer, chief stage technician, head of sound, production manager, systems engineer, twelve directors, seven designers, as well as the cast and associate artists. The scale is unique; many of these jobs do not exist as separate jobs in other theatres and, on a much smaller scale, have to be done by one person.

Producer

This is a post that exists in the commercial theatre; in a subsidised company many of the producer's duties are done by the artistic director or administrator. Producers shoulder the economic and managerial problems of putting on a play; they choose the play, rent the theatre, engage the director and stars and are responsible for paying all the bills

THEATRE

from the rent, rates and insurance to the salaries of the staff. They have to raise the money to put the production on and, if box-office takings fall, decide when to close it. Although producers have to consider their backers, they can also express their personal taste in the kind of plays they manage. The personal qualities a producer needs include tact, persuasiveness, business acumen, a flair for organisation and an instinct for what will go in the theatre. There are no specific training courses for producers, but a university drama course (see pp 59-63) can be useful; some start their careers as actors, others as assistant producers.

Director
Directors have overall responsibility for the artistic side of a production and must conduct rehearsals and keep an eye on all the backstage and technical departments. They sometimes commission the scripts they use or devise them themselves. They discuss their ideas about the production – whom they want to appear in it, to design the sets, lighting and costumes etc – with the producer. Directors tend to have strong personalities; they are the people with the artistic ideas and have to put these over to the company. There may be no more than a month of rehearsals in which to mount a production. Most directors work freelance, moving around from production to production and employing an agent to find them work and handle their business affairs, but a few are resident members of a company. Once the play opens, their job is finished. They receive a fee for each production plus a share of the box-office takings while the production is running.

Some directors also take on the duties of artistic director, which include planning the season's programme and supervising the budget.

Directors should have a thorough grounding in drama and practical experience of the theatre. Some have a drama degree (or while at university took part in a lot of student productions), others began their careers as actors or stage managers, and every director needs a lively, inventive, imaginative intelligence. There are drama-school courses in directing. The Regional Theatre Young Director Scheme, a two-year training scheme run by the Independent Television Fund on behalf of all the Independent Television companies, is intended for men and women aged between 20 and 26 who have had some experience in professional or amateur theatre or the allied arts and who wish to become directors in the professional theatre (see Further Information, p 54).

Casting Director
Casting directors work with the producer and director on the casting of

a production. They keep extensive records of who has done what and liaise with agents who are trying to get work for their clients. They go regularly to drama school productions looking for new talent and spend a lot of time auditioning and interviewing hopefuls. They need to have an excellent memory for faces and an instinctive knowledge of who will be right for a certain part. There is also work for casting directors in the film and video industries and in broadcasting.

Designer (see also Chapter 13)
In a large-scale production the sets and costumes will be the work of separate designers, but more often one designer will be responsible for both. Designers work closely with directors, interpreting and sometimes helping to shape their ideas. They produce drawings of the sets and costumes from which the scenery and costume department staff work; they make a scale model of the sets, which they show to the cast at the first rehearsal, and mark out the rehearsal room or stage floor with chalk to guide the actors until the set is ready. Designers need to have a thorough knowledge of period settings and costumes and a sense of style and of what will look effective on stage, and they have to work within a budget. Designers should be versatile as they might have to design for the traditional picture-frame proscenium stage, arena stage, theatre-in-the-round or for an outdoor production. They usually work freelance and often become closely associated with one director. Costume designers need a thorough knowledge of fabrics and training in and experience of pattern cutting and sewing; most have worked in a wardrobe department. (See also pp 51-2.)

Most designers have completed a full-time art and design course. (Scene painting and design are included in stage management courses.) Special courses are run by the Bristol Old Vic Theatre School, Guildhall School of Music and Drama, the Royal Academy of Dramatic Art (RADA), the Slade School of Fine Art, Riverside Studios, the Central School of Art and Design, City of Birmingham Polytechnic, Trent Polytechnic and Wimbledon School of Art. There is a CNAA BA (Hons) course in three-dimensional design (theatre design) at Trent Polytechnic, London Central School of Art and Design, and Wimbledon School of Art. It is also possible to study on an approved course for a BTEC award. There is a BTEC ND course in stage/design construction at Oldham College of Technology; a BTEC ND course in design (theatre studies) at Medway College of Design, Northbrook College of Design and Technology; a BTEC HND design (theatre studies) course at Croydon College, Mabel Fletcher Technical College, Liverpool,

Central School of Speech and Drama, London College of Fashion, and courses leading to college awards in theatre design at Croydon College, Northbrook College of Design and Technology. GCE A level craft (design and practice): syllabus B stage decor and costume courses are offered at North Tyneside College of Further Education and Nelson and Colne College; GCE A level courses in theatre design are offered at Colchester Institute, Barking College of Technology and Dacorum College.

Stage Manager
Stage managers and their team make sure that rehearsals and performances run smoothly. Stage managers usually have assistants (ASMs), who in small companies are sometimes asked to play minor parts or to understudy. Rehearsals are organised in consultation with the director; the stage manager sees that actors know when they are needed for rehearsal, makes notes of any changes in the script, of all the moves and actions of the actors, of scene changes, sound effects and when to ring up or lower the curtain. One of the ASMs will have the job of prompting during rehearsals and at the performance. The ASMs also keep an eye on the props and see that they are available at every performance. The stage manager of a large theatre or opera house may have to use sophisticated technical equipment.

Most drama-school courses include a certain amount of practical stage management. Course applicants are seldom required to have formal educational qualifications but will be expected to have had some backstage experience. There is usually an interview. There are courses in stage management at the Bristol Old Vic Theatre School, the Central School of Speech and Drama, Guildhall School of Music and Drama, the London Academy of Music and Dramatic Art, Middlesex Polytechnic, the Royal Academy of Dramatic Art, the Royal Scottish Academy of Music and Drama.

The kind of qualities that stage managers need include intelligence, practical ability, artistic flair, a certain authority, tact and an eye for detail. Stage managers often start their careers as ASMs, sometimes as actors.

The *stage crew* is a team of *scene-shifters*, whose work requires physical strength and split-second timing. The best way to get started in backstage work is to go along to a theatre and knock on the door; scene-shifters, *carpenters*, and *scene-painters* are often willing to take on an extra hand and are more impressed by obvious enthusiasm and love of the theatre than by formal qualifications. The mateyness of backstage life disposes those in charge to take on newcomers whom they feel will fit in. The best way to learn this kind of work is by doing it.

Lighting Director
In a large theatre with sophisticated equipment there will be a lighting director and a team of lighting electricians. The director will design the lighting plan and the team will rig the lights and operate them during the performance. In a small theatre one person may be in sole charge. Appropriate electrician qualifications are required for this work. Paddington College runs a theatre electricians' course and the Royal Academy of Dramatic Art a stage electrics course. There is City and Guilds 181 (Special) Theatre electricians.

Sound Manager
The sound manager makes the noises off and electronic effects, provides music (when there are no live performers) and tries to solve any acoustical problems. Training for this work is often acquired on the job.

House Manager
House managers look after the theatre, oversee its day-to-day running and maintenance. They supervise ushers/usherettes, programme sellers, cleaning, catering and security staff and are responsible for everything to do with the comfort and well-being of the audience. They are on duty during a performance to deal with any problems that might arise. The job, which does not require any stage training, could be a first step to a career in arts administration (see Chapter 15). House managers also work in concert halls, cinemas and arts centres. They need to be practical, well organised, tactful and calm. There is a college-based course in front of house studies at Neath College, and short in-service training courses for managers of small-scale professional theatre companies at the Independent Theatre Council, London.

Box Office Manager
The box office manager is in charge of the sale of tickets and is sometimes involved in promotion and marketing. Box office managers may have to fix terms for block bookings and agree allocations of seats with agencies, hotels and theatre clubs. Box office staff have to deal with personal bookings and with bookings made over the telephone and a lot of pressure can be put on them when a show is very popular. No formal training is needed but experience of accounts or general management would be useful.

Press/Publicity Officer

Publicity plans have to be made well in advance of the opening night. Publicity officers prepare press releases, arrange for actors and directors to be interviewed, invite critics to first nights, commission photographers and set up displays in the theatre foyer. They supervise the production of posters, mailing leaflets and programmes. An arts degree plus secretarial training would be a good preparation for this work. Theatre press officers can move into other sorts of PR work (see Chapter 10).

Education Officer

A theatre which has a theatre-in-education company attached to it may employ an education officer who will liaise with schools and colleges and organise performances, workshops, talks and backstage visits. A drama degree and/or teaching experience would be useful preparation for this work.

Production Staff

In a large company like the National Theatre, there is a series of production workshops each with its own speciality, but this scale of operation is rare. Many theatrical productions have few props and little scenery. Those whose jobs are outlined below could work in the theatre, opera, ballet, television or films.

Armourers make armour, weapons and items of decorative metalwork, and produce special effects, eg gunfire. Those who do this kind of work tend to be experts, eg gunsmiths, with a strong interest in period armour and costume.

Carpenters and joiners interpret the set designer's drawings and construct sets and items such as furniture for use on sets. Most of these things are dismantled after use. The Royal Academy of Dramatic Art, Hammersmith and West London College, run a course in theatrical carpentry.

A large company employs in-house *craftspeople*, eg plumbers, to carry out routine installation and maintenance tasks. There is a course leading to a college advanced diploma in theatre/television design and crafts at Northbrook College of Design and Technology.

Scenic artists and painters work under the set designer and paint sets, backcloths, gauzes. They often have to fake effects, eg a Roman arch, made of wood, must appear to be made of marble. Some of the work of a scenic artist is very skilled and applicants for such posts need a degree in fine art painting as well as a thorough knowledge of styles in architecture, painting and furniture. Scene painters' work is less skilled. The Guildhall School of Music and Drama runs a college course in scene painting and there is a RADA college award: diploma in scene painting and design.

Property staff (also known as 'props') provide all the movable items on a set – anything from an armchair to an ashtray. Some stage props, eg cigarettes, are donated by a manufacturer and there will be an acknowledgement on a theatre programme; sometimes they are bought from (or loaned by) antique dealers; sometimes they are specially made and the skills needed to do this can range from wood turning to upholstery. Members of an audience scrutinise props and do not hesitate to point out anachronisms and other mistakes. Property staff should have sound period knowledge and an eye for detail. They usually enjoy tracking down the items they need and are good improvisers when they cannot find what they want.

Costumes, wigs and accessories are often hired from theatrical costumiers, but a large theatre, opera, ballet or television company will have its own collection of garments and will employ cutters and assistants, hiring casual help when a big production is mounted. In addition to making costumes, *wardrobe staff* do fittings, alterations, mending, cleaning, laundering and stock checking. They are kept exceptionally busy when the company goes on tour. There are theatre wardrobe courses run by the Bristol Old Vic Theatre School, the London College of Fashion, Mabel Fletcher Technical College, Wimbledon School of Art, Sandown College, Bournemouth and Poole College of Art and Design.

Make-up Artist

Most actors learn make-up at drama school and, when acting in the theatre, like to do their own, but in television and films, where so many shots are in close up, it is usually done by a make-up artist. In television, make-up artists spend much of their time doing corrective work, combing and lacquering hair and powdering noses and foreheads. The creative side comes from drama and light entertainment productions for which they may have to do elaborate face and body make-up and produce special effects such as scars and bruises. Make-up artists do not always find themselves in the comparative comfort of a studio or dressing room; location work may take them outside in bad weather. They need a calm, tactful personality for they work with many different sorts of people – actors, politicians, ordinary members of the public – all of whom are likely to be nervous just before going on camera or on stage. Courses are run by Bournemouth and Poole College of Art and Design, Langley College, London College of Fashion, the BBC.

Work on wigs and beards may be done by wardrobe staff or make-up staff or, in a very large company, by the staff of a special department. City and Guilds 301 wig-making is widely available in England and Wales and there are courses available at Kirby College of Further Education leading to a regional award in applied commercial and theatrical haircraft.

Job Opportunities

You will find the jobs outlined above all over the UK – with regional theatre, opera and ballet companies and with television companies. There are some regular, salaried posts but freelance staff are frequently hired for a specific production (and there cannot always be any guarantee how long this will last). Jobs are advertised in the quality press, *Time Out* and *Stage and Television Today*, and some London secretarial agencies specialise in media jobs. Often, the best way to find work is to apply in person at the theatre. Salaries in the theatre are seldom high.

Career Development

There is no such thing as a standard career path in the theatre. Experience gained in theatre, opera or ballet production will stand you in good stead when you apply for television work.

Personal Qualities

The theatre tends to attract people with strong and sometimes temperamental personalities. Nevertheless, a production of any kind is a team effort and a theatrical company is generally a close-knit community.

Entry Requirements and Training

This is an area where formal qualifications take second place to talent, experience and commitment. There are specific training courses and these are mentioned under the job headings.

Further Information

Always send a self-addressed stamped envelope.

Association of British Theatre Technicians (ABTT), 4-9 Great Pulteney Street, London W1R 3DF
Independent Television Association, 56 Mortimer Street, London W1N 8AN
Independent Theatre Council, Old Loom House, Backchurch Lane, London E1 1LU
Regional Theatre Young Director Scheme (write to RTYDS Administrator)
Royal Academy of Dramatic Art (RADA), 62 Gower Street, London W1R 3DF

British Alternative Theatre Directory (John Offord Publications)
British Theatre Directory (John Offord Publications in association with British Theatre Institute)
Careers in the Theatre (Kogan Page)
Contacts (published by Spotlight)
DATEC Directory of Drama Courses in Higher Education (British Theatre Institute)
Stage and Television Today

Chapter 4
Performers

Some people are happiest when they are on stage, in front of a camera or behind a microphone; they are 'performers'. The urge to perform is something you are born with and, it you have it, you will not be put off by warnings about overcrowding in the performing arts, cut-throat competition or the precariousness of the life. Performers can learn technique, but star quality, possessed by great performers, cannot be acquired. Very few make it to the top and no one, having got there, can be sure of remaining at the top. Most performers have a satisfying but unspectacular career, as for example, supporting actors, orchestral players, session singers/musicians, or members of the corps de ballet/chorus line and may eventually move on into a related field such as direction/production, teaching or agency work.

Union Membership
Members of the British Actors Equity Association (Equity) come from all branches of the entertainments industry and include actors, cabaret artists, choreographers, circus performers, dancers, directors, designers, ice skaters, singers, stage managers, stunt performers and variety artists. In most areas of the industry casting agreements have been made with employers which stipulate that only members of Equity (or an agreed quota of newcomers) are eligible for work. You cannot get a membership card unless you have been offered an Equity-approved contract or gained experience working as a provisional member. In normal circumstances, it will not be possible for you to obtain your first job and Equity membership in the West End theatre, the National Theatre, the larger summer seasons, pantomimes, tours, television, commercials, films or radio. Equity will provide a list of the types of engagement through which membership can be obtained.

Actor

The most obvious kind of performing is acting. Acting is the interpretation of an author's work and its communication to an audience; it is both a craft and an art form. At drama school you learn to use the tools of the trade, your body and your voice, but without that indefinable and unacquirable quality, stage presence, you will not be even modestly successful.

In the past, an actor set his/her sights on the stage or on the screen – few worked for both media; nowadays, despite the fact that the techniques of stage and screen acting are very different, almost all actors work in both media.

The openings in the theatre are as follows.

Subsidised Theatre (eg the National, the Royal Court)
Actors are initially hired for 60 weeks (ie one season) or for a single play which may stay in the repertoire for two to three years, and the director will decide whether or not to renew their contract.

Commercial Theatre
Actors are hired for a single play whose run may last months or only a few days. Backers, naturally, try to make a profit so productions tend to be of 'safe' pieces – musicals, thrillers or light comedies. Sometimes, during a long run, an actor will do other work during the day.

Repertory Companies
These are the companies in which, traditionally, young actors made their debut. There are about 70 repertory companies in the UK and they have very different policies; some cater for the tastes of a middle-aged, conservative audience, others perform a lot of new plays. Actors are engaged for a season.

Alternative and Fringe Companies
These are usually small – perhaps just half a dozen actors and a director who might have joined up at drama school – and work with minimum equipment. Some receive subsidies from regional arts associations or local authorities but most are run on a shoestring an the rewards are strictly in terms of job satisfaction. They tend to perform new and often experimental work which may have a strong political or social message. Fringe companies tour and can put on a show anywhere – in a club, pub or church hall – and occasionally one will gain a national reputation.

Community Theatre Companies
These seek to work with local people, running workshops and devising

dramatic happenings about local issues and topical matters. This is the theatre of those who see drama as a force for social change.

Theatre-in-Education
A number of repertory theatres have theatre-in-education companies attached to them which take productions to schools and colleges.

Children's Theatre
This ranges from long-established companies putting on several major productions a year to tiny touring companies. Programmes demand a mixture of skills, from mime and clowning to manipulating puppets, and usually involve some degree of audience participation through singing and playing games. Some take the form of workshops and encourage the children themselves to perform.

Other openings exist in:

Radio
Most radio plays are one-off productions, but actors can be offered contracts for daily, weekly or occasional serials. Actors are also used for prose and poetry readings.

Film
Actors are hired for a particular film; this will probably give them a few days' or weeks' work even though the whole production may take several months.

Television
Actors are hired for a particular programme which may be a one-off play or a long-running serial.

Television Commercials
These are made both by independent production companies and by well-known film directors. Actors are hired for a particular commercial, or series of commercials for the same product.

Those with a 'speciality' act (eg jugglers, stand-up comics, magicians) may find work in clubs, variety, pantomime or cabaret.

Working Conditions
Actors must expect periods of unemployment: 75 per cent of Equity's members are out of work at any one time and 4 per cent may 'rest' for an entire year. When they have work, they keep long, unsocial hours. In

the live theatre performances are in the evenings and usually on two afternoons a week, and in repertory actors might be rehearsing one play during the day and performing in another in the evening. Rehearsals can last weeks, if not months, for a production which may have only a very limited run. Film and television productions have tight schedules and it is not uncommon to have to be on the set at 7 am. The work involves hours, sometimes days, of waiting around in full make-up and costume for short intensive bursts of action.

Job Opportunities

Acting is the most overcrowded profession in the world and actors nearly always need a second source of income. Contacts are very important to actors. Personal contacts are fine as far as they go, but actors need an agent (see p 157) who will 'sell' them to directors and producers, negotiate their contracts and arrange their publicity. Agents also learn about forthcoming productions long before news of them becomes public. It is also a good idea to advertise in *Spotlight*. Theatrical agents are concentrated in London and the south east but there are theatres and theatrical companies all over the UK and you must be prepared to go to where the jobs are. Work can take you anywhere, from Tyne and Wear to Thailand, and the stories about theatrical digs are notorious.

Career Development

Traditionally, the ideal progress for a young actor is to start in repertory, get some experience of television and film, and then join a major company or break into the commercial theatre. One of the things a good agent will do is advise a client about his/her career and, occasionally, this advice will be to turn down a part; it can greatly harm an actor's image to be miscast or typecast. Actors usually have to audition for a part and you should have a number of prepared, contrasting audition pieces.

In order to be able to work in all areas of the profession you need to be a full member of the actors' union, Equity (see p 55).

Starting Salaries

Minimum weekly salaries set by Equity are: £112 for repertory, £130 for provincial commercial, £138 for fringe, £145 for London West End. Equity have a number of different arrangements for television and film work, all of which is better paid than stage work.

PERFORMERS

Personal Qualities
The work is physically taxing and mentally demanding and the life precarious so actors need considerable stamina. They must also be intelligent, receptive to direction and able to work in a team with other members of the cast. Despite its obvious drawbacks, the work is uniquely satisfying and few actors would contemplate doing anything else.

Entry Requirements and Training
There are no minimum educational qualifications demanded of actors; however, most go through drama school and, as there is stiff competition for places, applicants with O or A levels (or equivalent) have the edge over others.

Most acting courses last at least two years, at the end of which the college or school awards its own diploma. The content and emphasis of the courses vary from school to school, but the aim is the same: to teach students how to use their voice, body and imagination. Most schools have their own theatre(s) and put on productions in a number of styles. Students get a chance to show what they have learned in full-length productions, and these are particularly important in the final year, when agents and casting directors are looking out for promising new talent. Students are also given audition practice, and most schools provide training in radio and television techniques, some in specially equipped studios.

The following schools offer courses which have been accredited by the National Council for Drama Training: Academy of Live and Recorded Arts, London; Arts Educational Schools, London; Birmingham School of Speech Training and Dramatic Art; Bristol Old Vic Theatre School; Central School of Speech and Drama, London; Drama Centre, London; Drama Studio, London; Guildford School of Acting and Drama Dance Education; Guildhall School of Music and Drama, London; London Academy of Music and Dramatic Art; Manchester Polytechnic School of Theatre; Middlesex Polytechnic; Mountview Theatre School; Rose Bruford College of Speech and Drama, Sidcup, Royal Academy of Dramatic Art, London; Royal Scottish Academy of Dramatic Art, Glasgow; Webber Douglas Academy of Dramatic Art, London; Welsh College of Music and Drama, Cardiff.

University First Degrees
BA Hons combined subjects Drama; BA Special Hons Drama and theatre arts;

CAREERS IN THE MEDIA

Music, drama and dance, Birmingham
BA Drama, Bristol
BA Hons Drama, East Anglia
BA Combined Hons German-drama; BA Hons Drama; English and drama, Exeter
BA Ord Dramatic studies, MA Ord/Hons and MA (Soc Sci) Ord/Hons Theatre studies, Glasgow
BA Hons Drama; BA Special Hons Drama, Hull
BA Hons Drama; Drama-theatre studies, Kent
BA Combined Hons, English-theatre studies; BA Hons, Theatre studies, Lancaster
BA Combined Hons, Drama-English, London Goldsmiths' C
BA Hons, Drama-theatre studies, London Royal Holloway and Bedford C
BA Hons Combined studies, Classical studies-Drama; English-drama, London Westfield C
BA Drama, English and drama, Loughborough
BA Hons Drama; English and drama; French and drama; German and drama, Manchester
BA Hons Humanities Combined theatre studies, Ulster
BA Hons Drama, BA Joint Hons Drama, Wales, Aberystwyth
BA Hons (with Qualified Teacher status) Drama; BA Hons English-theatre studies; Theatre studies and dramatic arts, Warwick

CNAA Polytechnic Degree
BA/BA Hons Drama, Liverpool

Higher Degrees awarded by Universities
MPhil (Arts) Drama, Birmingham
MA Drama studies; French drama and theatre history, Bristol
MPhil French theatre studies, Glasgow
MA Theatre and media production, Hull
MA, MSc, LLM, Drama, Kent
MA, MSc Theatre studies; French theatre studies; MPhil, LLM Theatre studies, Lancaster
MA and MA (Collegiate) Theatre studies, Leeds
PhD, MPhil, Drama, London Goldsmiths' C
MA Drama-theatre studies, London Royal Holloway and Bedford C
MPhil Drama, Manchester
MA Theatre studies, Southampton
MA English and European Renaissance drama, Warwick

PERFORMERS

Higher Degrees awarded by Polytechnics
BA Dramatic studies, Royal Scottish

Diplomas awarded by Universities
University Diploma Drama, Kent
Drama, Manchester
Drama in education, Nottingham
Drama, Wales

Diplomas awarded by Polytechnics
Polytechnic Diploma Theatre, Manchester
Polytechnic Diploma Dramatic art, Middlesex
College Diploma Drama, Queen Margaret

Certificates awarded by Universities
Drama, Bristol
Certificate Literature and drama, London Goldsmiths' C
Extra-mural Certificate and Diploma Drama and theatre studies, London
Extra-Mural Studies Dept

Certificates awarded by Polytechnics
Polytechnic Certificate Stage management and technical theatre, Middlesex
Postgraduate CNAA Certificate, Drama, Middlesex

CNAA
BA Hons in Drama, theatre and television studies, King Alfred's C, Winchester
BA Hons in Theatre, Dartington CA
BA Hons in Theatre arts, Rose Bruford CSp&D
BEd/BEd Hons in Speech and drama, North London Poly
University of Lancaster BA Hons in Drama and a minor subject, Liverpool Poly
University of Leeds BA Hons in Drama, Bretton Hall C
University of London Certificate in Drama and theatre studies, City Lit
University of Wales BEd Hons in Drama, South Glamorgan IHE, Welsh CM&D
Combined subjects degree, Drama option, Bedford CHE, Nene C, Northampton,
Goldsmiths' C, Middlesex Poly, Roehampton IHE, St Mary's C,

Twickenham, West London IHE, Chester C, Crewe + Alsager CHE, Liverpool IHE, Liverpool Poly, Worcester CHE, Bedford CHE, Middlesex Poly
Combined subjects degree: Drama, film and television option, Ripon and York, St John C
Combined subjects degree: Drama and theatre craft option, North Cheshire C
Combined subjects degree: Film and drama option, Bulmershe CHE
Combined subjects degree: Theatre arts option, Rolle C, Exeter
Combined subjects degree: Theatre studies option, Wolverhampton Poly, Poly of Wales,
Creative/performing arts degree: Drama option, Trent Poly, Middlesex Poly
Performing arts degree: Leicester Poly
Guildhall School of Music and Drama, Licentiate diploma, acting, Guildhall
SM&D, Highbury CT (Portsmouth), Stoke Cauldon CF&HE
London Academy of Music and Dramatic Art, Acting diploma, East Surrey C, Redhill
Royal Society of Arts, Diploma in drama and theatre arts, Havering CAdE
SCOTVEC NC modules, Drama, Kirkcaldy CT, Inverness CF&HE

College Awards
Certificate in creative arts (drama), City and East London C
Certificate in drama and visual arts, Northampton CFE
Certificate in dramatic arts and related studies, Telford CFE
Advanced certificate in drama, Welsh CM&D
Certificate in performance arts, Shirecliffe C, Sheffield
Certificate in performance arts (advanced), Laban CM&D
Certificate in theatre arts, Redbridge TC, South Warwickshire CFE
Certificate in theatre studies/Advanced certificate in theatre studies, South Cheshire C
Diploma in acting, Central SS&D, LAMDA, ADA
Diploma in community theatre arts, Rose Bruford CS&D, Ulster U
Diploma in drama, Highbury CT, Portsmouth, Queen Margaret C, Edinburgh, Havering TC, Hornchurch
Diploma in drama (acting) Highbury CT, Portsmouth
Diploma in drama (stage management and crafts), Highbury CT, Portsmouth
Diploma in drama and television studies, Southampton TC

Diploma in dramatic art, Middlesex Poly, Royal SAMD
Diploma in performance arts, Farnborough CT, Shirecliffe C, Sheffield
Diploma in speech and drama, Weston super Mare TC&SA
Diploma in theatre studies, Sandown C
Diploma in technical theatre arts, Rose Bruford CSp&D
Graduate diploma in drama, Welsh CM&D
Licentiate diploma in drama (performer), Welsh CM&D, Cardiff

College-based Courses
Advanced course in speech and drama, Central SSp&D
Course(s) in theatre in theatre and performing arts, East Herts C, Harrogate CAT
Drama performance skill, Harlow C
Dramatic art, Charles Keene CFE, Leicester, Doncaster MetIHE

Further information
See end of chapter, page 69.

Stunt Performer

Stunt performers are filmed doing such things as leaping out of upper-floor windows with their clothes on fire or driving cars over precipices. It is skilled and dangerous work which needs split-second timing. Stunt performers provide their own equipment and work with a trusted technician. A film script may call for the skills of a number of stunt performers each with his/her own speciality. Top actors all have stunt doubles, who must be able to act well enough to look convincing as the star. A film producer will not let a star risk breaking a leg during shooting and will insist on using a double for the risky bits.

Stunt performers must get themselves on to the Register of Stunt Performers and Arrangers and there is a three-year probationary period. Full members of the Register can become stunt arrangers and set up stunts for other performers. It can take many years to become a topline stunt arranger. The overheads are very high: basic equipment, eg a fire suit, is expensive and so are insurance premiums.

Job Opportunities
The work is surprisingly popular and there is considerable competition for jobs; it can take you all over the world as, of course, a lot of it is done

on location. Stunt performers work freelance and need an agent (see p 157).

Career Development
As stunt performers may work as seldom as twice a year, most of them have an alternative source of income. They rarely continue working after the age of 30.

Entry Requirements
Stunt performers need acting ability and must be Equity members. They should be proficient in: fencing, judo, aikido, wrestling, other martial arts, boxing, falling, trampolining, diving, parachuting, riding and driving horses/motorcars/motorbikes, gymnastics, and swimming.

Personal Characteristics
This work calls for peak physical fitness, excellent body co-ordination and a cool head. Stunt performers must know exactly what the risks are and plan each stunt meticulously; this is not a job for careless daredevils.

Dancer, Choreographer

There are three main kinds of dance: Ballet, contemporary dance and modern dance. Modern dance includes jazz and tap dancing, disco and acrobatics. Rather more opportunities exist in modern dance than in ballet or contemporary dance. Modern dance practitioners may find themselves working in musical stage shows, television, films, cabaret or pantomime. Modern dance is a less demanding discipline than ballet; nevertheless, rehearsals and practice take up a great deal of a dancer's time.

Choreographers, who create and arrange dance sequences, need an imaginative understanding which is usually gained from years of experience of music and dance. Some choreographers start out as dancers or dance teachers; some take specialist courses in the subject.

Personal Qualities
Dancers must be hard-working, mentally and physically self-disciplined, dedicated, determined and healthy. They must also be the right height, shape and size, graceful, well poised and attractive. The work calls for imagination, a good sense of timing and an ear for music.

PERFORMERS

Job Opportunities
The best way to find work is through an agent (see p 157). In the commercial theatre dancers are hired for a particular show, which may run for a few days or several months. At the time of writing a lot of musicals are running – they are considered a 'safe' form of commercial theatre – so there are more job opportunities than there have been for several years. There are some permanent dance troupes which are hired for stage, television and television commercial work.

Career Prospects
Successful dancers have to make a name early as few continue to dance after the age of 40.

Starting Salary
Salaries vary from company to company but should not be lower than £112 per week.

Entry Requirements and Training
There are no minimum educational requirements; entry to a dance school is almost invariably by audition. However, as nearly all dancers need to take other work in order to survive it is a good idea to acquire some educational qualifications.

Ideally, ballet students should attend a recognised, residential establishment from the age of 11. It is essential to undergo formal training in order to perform as a professional and there are a range of specialist courses available.

The following schools offer courses accredited by the Council for Dance Education and Training: Arts Education Trust School, London; Ballet Rambert School, Twickenham; Brooking School of Ballet, London; Bush Davies School, East Grinstead; Central School of Ballet, London; Doreen Bird College, Sidcup; Elmhurst Ballet School, Camberley; Hammond School, Chester; Italia Conti Academy of Theatre Arts, London; Laban Centre for Movement and Dance, London; Laine Theatre Arts, Epsom; Legat School, Crowborough; London Contemporary Dance School, London; London College of Dance and Drama, Bedford.

Further Information
See end of chapter.

CAREERS IN THE MEDIA

Musician

There are some salaried posts for musicians with orchestras, chamber groups and choirs. The BBC is the biggest employer of salaried musicians. Most musicians are freelance and find work through an agent (see p 158). When musicians have work they may keep long, unsocial hours and do a lot of travelling.

Job Opportunities
Work is not very plentiful and nearly all performers try to do as much session work as possible.

Entry Requirements
No minimum educational qualifications are required of performers; however, most applicants who audition for performers' courses hold GCSEs, O or A levels (or equivalent). Performers must normally be members of a union: instrumentalists belong to the Musicians' Union and singers to Equity.

Personal Qualities
As musical standards are very high and competition is keen, only very talented musicians can make a career as a performer. The work is physically and mentally taxing and the lifestyle hard so musicians need considerable resilience. Good hearing, the ability to sightread and master nerves are essential, and singers are considerably helped by attractive looks and personality.

Further Information
See end of chapter.

Model

Most models are freelances and rely on an agent to find them work (see p 156). The fashion industry is the main source of live work. At the top of the market are the *haute couture* collections which take place in March and October. These are lavish productions attended by the fashion press, other designers and buyers. There is seasonal showroom and exhibition work with wholesale fashion warehouses and with large shops and stores. Show models can be divided into several categories: the good all-rounders; those who specialise in high fashion and photographic work;

and those who appear in the very specialised choreographed shows. All good show models must be at least 5ft 7in (170cm) tall. Whatever the type of show work, there will be auditions, bookings and days of fittings and rehearsal.

Photographic modelling is the toughest and most competitive side of the business. Advertising forms the largest part of the photographic model's work. Advertisements can be seen in newspapers and magazines, on hoardings, on public transport, in public places such as railway stations and airports, in shops. Models of all kinds are used in advertisements: chubby babies, spry pensioners, 'ordinary' folk and exotic types. Television and film commercials are made by both models and by actors and to do this kind of work models are granted temporary Equity membership (see p 55).

Editorial work is considered the best kind of photographic assigment; modelling shoes, fashions, hair-styles or make-up in the editorial pages of a magazine or posing for illustrations to go with articles and stories. There is a very wide range of magazines, from the top fashion glossies through those produced weekly for the housewife and mother, the working girl-about-town, the teenager and the senior citizen. There are also special interest publications on, for example, sport, health, slimming, physical fitness, knitting, sewing, cookery.

Catalogue work, which is seasonal, is well paid but generally unpopular with models.

Glamour work is not to every model's taste; it involves posing nude or semi-nude for calendars and pin-ups. It must be stressed that this work does not include posing for pornographic magazines.

Male Model

There is now more of a demand for male models and most of the assignments are for photographic modelling. Male models must be at least 5ft 11in (180 cm) tall.

Mature Model

For a woman the peak years for fashion modelling are between 17 and 30 and for photographic modelling from 16 to 25. However, there is scope in the 30-45 age range for both men and women and sometimes models are able to use their own children in family advertisements. Casting agents are on the look-out for men with mature looks for the big money advertisements for spirits, cars and tobacco. Catalogue work is a good source of employment for the older model and there is an increasing number of magazines aimed at the retired reader.

Personal Qualities

The ideal measurements for a female model are height between 5ft 7in (170 cm) and 5ft 10in (178 cm), bust 34B (86 cm), waist 24-25in (60 cm), hips 35-36in (89 cm), and for the male model are minimum height 5ft 11 in (180 cm), chest 40in (101 cm), waist 31in (79 cm), hips 38in (96 cm), inside leg 34in (86 cm). All models must have reasonable looks, even features, good teeth, a blemish free complexion, a well-proportioned body and strong healthy hair. It is important to keep in good physical condition.

Models of all types are needed. The more versatile you are, the more work you will find and it is useful to be able to dance, swim, skate, ride a horse/bicycle. Above all, you must be photogenic and come alive in front of the camera. You should have a thoroughly professional attitude to your work and, in the early years, you must have the courage to weather periods of little or no work and to bear the disappointment of being turned down at an audition.

Starting Salary

Starting salaries are low but an experienced model can earn in the region of £20,000 a year.

Entry Requirements and Training

There are varying opinions within the industry on the merits or otherwise of training schools and courses. Generally, agents today prefer to train new recruits themselves. If you decide to take a course at a school, make your choice carefully. Anyone can open a school purporting to teach modelling; there are no prescribed standards to which such schools have to conform and fees can be very high. Find out how long the school has been established and what its tutors' qualifications are. Ask about the success rate of previous students and what work they are doing now. A good school will be honest about your chances of success.

A number of schools are linked to an agency thus combining the best of both worlds and these schools only accept students whom they feel able to place on their books at the end of the course.

The only accredited school in the country is the London College of Fashion and its course, which runs from September to July, is the only full-time course. There is very keen competition for the 32 places and applicants should have a minimum of three O levels (or equivalent). Students who successfully complete the course are awarded the College's certificate in fashion modelling.

Other Openings for Performers

Announcer, radio and television (see p 17)

Media Personality
There is already a great deal of radio and television airtime to fill and in the 1990s there will be even more. Chat shows, quizzes, panel games and features proliferate and there is a continuous demand for people to take part in these programmes. Almost anyone who becomes well known in his/her own field – and this could be anything from industry to the Church – and who has the right personality may be invited to take part in a radio or television programme. If the first appearance is successful, other invitations will follow and in no time a new 'media personality' is born. Actors, in particular, find this kind of work usefully lucrative; however, they have to be careful not to become over-exposed or to accept the kind of assignment that would harm their image.

Music Presenter (disc jockey/DJ), radio (see p 21)

News Reader (news presenter, newscaster and anchorman/woman), radio and television (see p 22)

Programme Presenter, radio and television (see p 22)

Further Information (including job advertisements)

Always send a self-addressed stamped envelope.

British Actors Equity Association, 8 Harley Street, London W1N 2AB
Musicians Union, 60-62 Clapham Road, London SW9 0JJ
National Council for Drama Training and Council for Dance Education and Training, 5 Tavistock Place, London WC1H 9SS
Scottish Council for Dance, PO Box 410 WDO, Edinburgh EH12 6AR
Dance Council for Wales, The Torch Theatre, At Peters Road, Milford Haven, Dyfed
Spotlight, Charles House, 7 Leicester Place, London WC2H 7BP

CAREERS IN THE MEDIA

British Theatre Directory and *British Alternative Theatre Directory* (John Offord Publications)
Campaign
Careers in Classical Music (Kogan Page)
Careers in Modelling (Kogan Page)
Careers in the Music Business (Kogan Page)
Careers in Television and Radio (Kogan Page)
Careers in the Theatre (Kogan Page)
Contacts (published by Spotlight)
DATEC Directory of Drama Courses in Higher Education (British Theatre Institute)
Drama and Dance, Choice of Careers No 98 (HMSO)
Kemps International Music and Recording Yearbook
The Listener
Showcall
The Stage

Chapter 5
Journalism

In journalism you can be either salaried or freelance and the three main areas of work are: the press (provincial, national and agencies), periodicals and broadcasting. There is a great deal of job mobility in journalism; newspaper journalism is a long-established career in its own right but many people use it as a springboard to enter broadcasting. For press photography and photojournalism, see p 144.

Newspapers

Reporters
Reporters are sent on assignments or nose out their own stories by following up leads or receiving tip-offs from contacts. Before going to cover a story, they will try to get as much background information as possible from the newspaper's library and on-line data service and may try to set up interviews. When some unexpected newsworthy event, eg a serious accident, occurs there is no time to do any preparation and they simply try to get on the scene as quickly as possible. They write up their piece and deliver or fax the copy, or phone in the story, by the deadline. At the last minute any story, however good, may be drastically cut or spiked (rejected) because another more important story has broken and has to be given priority coverage. Reporters are employed by national newspapers, local and provincial newspapers and freesheets and the events they cover can be anything from a political assassination to a local wedding. The majority work on local and provincial newspapers, of which there are approximately 1000 dailies or weeklies. The provincial press gives priority to local news and puts a local slant on national/international news, and its reporters are less specialised than those of the national press.

Columnists
Columnists, as their name suggests, have a regular signed column in

which they write about a subject from their own point of view, very often a political point of view.

Correspondents
Foreign correspondents cover foreign news stories; they may be based abroad or sent abroad to cover, for example, a local war or an election. Other correspondents cover such things as political news, court and social events, sport, City news.

Feature Writers
Feature writers produce articles which are longer than news stories and need not necessarily be hotly topical; for example, they conduct and write up in-depth interviews or supply regular pieces on such subjects as wine, food, gardening, fashion or DIY. Like all journalists, they have to meet deadlines, but they usually have enough time to do thorough background research and know how many words they have to produce.

Critics
Critics review books, films, plays, television and radio programmes, records etc. On a provincial newspaper, a reporter may do some reviewing.

Sub Editors
Sub editors (subs) spike, cut, and occasionally rewrite, articles produced by other journalists. They deal with continuing stories which come in a bit at a time and, on provincial papers, write up notes sent in by club secretaries. They write headlines and, in between editions, may update stories or change page layout. On a large newspaper a sub editor may be in charge of just one page, eg a sports page.

Chief Editors
Chief editors are responsible for the policy and overall content of the publication.

Production Editors
Production editors are in charge of page layout and decide on which page a story will appear.

All journalists must be able to type and write shorthand (100 wpm) and, as many newspapers are now composed and printed electronically, must be familiar with and able to use the new technology. Nowadays journalists generally work with a wordprocessor (which will conveniently check spelling and count words) and send in their copy over the telephone via a fax.

Periodicals

There are approximately 7500 periodicals published in the UK; they include the large circulation titles which are to be found on newsagents' shelves, house magazines intended for the staff of the organisations which produce them, professional publications intended for, for example, doctors, lawyers, teachers, trade magazines covering such subjects as grocery, tourism, leisure, and magazines producted by or for, for example, cultural, social, scientific organisations and associations. There is hardly a subject you can think of which does not have a periodical covering it. Learned journals are usually published by book publishers. Some periodicals are little more than news-sheets but many are well-produced, substantial publications employing full-time writers and editors and the magazines that make use of colour printing and art work employ design staff.

Magazine journalists work to deadlines that are just as strict as those that operate in newspapers, but they have longer to research their stories, usually know how many words they must produce, and seldom have their work spiked.

Radio and Television

Radio/television reporters, like newspaper reporters, will try to gather as much background information as they can before going out to cover a story. They work under a great deal of pressure as a lot of their time is spent reporting hot news. A radio reporter may simply go out alone with a tape recorder; a television reporter will be accompanied by a camera and lighting crew. The big broadcasting organisations employ correspondents, who specialise in such subjects as politics or industrial relations, to provide in-depth coverage of important issues and they have foreign correspondents based abroad in major capitals.

News bulletins are broadcast live and usually consist of prepared script, edited tapes, live or recorded interviews and on-the-spot live coverage. News editors, who work in the newsroom, decide on the content of a bulletin and the weighting of the various items that make it up, and write a lot of the material. Radio and television news staff work under immense pressure; there are the strict deadlines imposed by programme schedules and news is continually changing – new stories break and items have to be updated. Magazine programmes are produced at a more leisurely pace, reporters can usually edit their own tapes and there is seldom any live reporting.

Other Types of Journalism

Press Agencies
The press agencies, eg Reuters, provide a reporting service, press cuttings and photographs, for newspapers and broadcasting organisations; they employ journalists, feature writers and may have branches all over the world.

Government Press Services
The government's own publishing house, Her Majesty's Stationery Office, in its various ministerial and press offices employs journalists who carry out a number of tasks: writing, sub editing, issuing press releases, arranging interviews and press conferences, and making films.

Work Settings

Reporters work in the field. Those who cover local or regional news are unlikely to have to travel outside a radius of 50 miles and much of their time will be spent sitting in council chambers or magistrates' courts, attending weddings and flower shows and waiting for the big story to break. Journalists employed by national newspapers or broadcasting organisations may cover hundreds of miles a week and can expect to be sent abroad, occasionally to dangerous trouble spots, at short notice. In a news room there will be journalists sitting at computer terminals inputting stories, sub editors writing headlines and processing stories as they come in, news editors writing stories for broadcast bulletins, editing audio or videotape. News typists will be typing bulletins or taking dictation straight on to the keyboard.

Very few newspaper, television or radio journalists work from nine to five; many have to endure long periods of waiting between periods of intense activity. There may be evening, weekend or shift work. In the editorial office of a periodical, the atmosphere will be less tense as journalists do not have to process hot news.

Job Opportunities

There is work to be found all over the UK; most towns of any size have a local newspaper and/or freesheet, and there are regional television stations and companies, BBC and independent local radio stations, and soon there will be community radio. Certain jobs are concentrated in or around London – those with the national newspapers and with book or magazine publishers. New jobs are being created all the time – some ventures are very short-lived – and there is keen competition in all parts of the industry. Jobs are advertised in the quality press, the *Listener*, the *Bookseller*, *UK Press Gazette*, *Media Week*, *Campaign*.

Freelance Work

Freelance journalist have to find a market for their own work. They may: a) supply by arrangement (as to subject matter, number of words, rate of pay etc) a single contribution or series of contributions to a newspaper, magazine or television or radio station; b) write or record a story/article/feature etc and then seek to place it; c) become a regular contributor; d) supply regularly or intermittently, for agreed rates of pay, specialised articles or recorded items on a given subject.

Freelance journalists do not have to have any particular educational qualifications nor are they obliged to belong to any union or trade association, have any journalistic certificates or have served an apprenticeship. Those who are NUJ members can seek the NUJ's help in negotiating full NUJ rates of pay.

It is possible to make a good living as a freelance provided you have a certain amount of regular work, but you have to cultivate your contacts, keep up to date in your field (read, keep your eyes and ears open) and come up with new angles to stories and fresh approaches, and look for new outlets for your work.

Personal Qualities

Journalists work with words so must have an excellent command of English; radio and television journalists, of course, need fluent spoken as well as written English and a good microphone (and camera) manner. They must work fast and accurately while under pressure: copy must be filed on time (radio and television journalists can expect to do live reporting) and must generally be of a precise length. Good reporters are interested in current affairs (local, national and international), people, places and events and they have a nose for a story and are resourceful when it comes to pursuing a lead. Frequently, they have to be able to seize on what is essential, eg in a long interview or political speech, and present it succinctly condensed. In order to get the best out of interviewees journalists must know how to put them at their ease while at the same time coming straight to the point with the right questions. Journalists must know, and be able to write appropriately for, their readership; for example, what was comprehensible and interesting to readers of the *Guardian*'s financial pages would not be suitable for those seeking financial enlightenment from the *Sun*.

Getting Started

Aspiring journalists cannot begin too soon. Learn to type and write shorthand (and to use a tape recorder if you have set your sights on radio) and start writing for, or editing, your school or college magazine and send in contributions to your local newspaper or radio station so that when you have your first job interview you will have samples of your work to show. Editors of local newspapers occasionally allow young people wanting to enter journalism to spend a few days with a reporter as an observer. This is an excellent way to get the feel of the job.

It is very rare for any journalist to start his/her career with a national newspaper; most people under the age of 24 apply for a direct-entry traineeship with a provincial newspaper. Most of those who apply for work in radio or television are experienced newspaper journalists. The BBC has a small intake of graduate trainees.

Career Development

Some journalists will move from newspaper work into broadcasting and, once in broadcasting, may move to and fro between radio and television. In newspaper journalism a cub reporter becomes a qualified senior, then may choose to specialise, eg in financial journalism, or become a columnist, leader writer or critic. On the editorial side, a sub editor can become a chief sub editor, assistant editor or editor. On the editorial side of periodical publishing an assistant editor progresses via copy-editing and desk editing to commissioning. Journalists can move

JOURNALISM

into other related areas of work; a financial journalist, for example, who may have come from the City in the first place, could move into merchant banking or consultancy work.

Starting Salaries

Salaries vary greatly. Trainees on a small weekly paper earn about £4000, whereas qualified journalists on a London daily can earn over £15,000. The recommended rate for freelance journalists is £80 per 1000 words.

Unions

The National Union of Journalists (NUJ) and the Institute of Journalists are both the principal professional organisations and the registered trade unions. Their members are in newspapers, news agencies, magazines, book publishing and public relations, and there is student membership.

Entry Requirements and Training

Newspapers

Training for reporters and press photographers is provided almost exclusively by the regional and local press. You will find the names of regional and local newspapers in *Benn's UK Media Directory* and *Willing's Press Guide*, copies of which are generally to be found in public libraries. Most newspaper companies are members of the Newspaper Society and they offer comprehensive training. The National Council for the Training of Journalists (NCTJ) regulates and administers the official scheme, which is a mix of course learning and structured in-company training. The course learning may be undertaken in block-release periods if the trainee is employed by a newspaper or in a one-year, full-time course, or on a postgraduate course. The accredited colleges offering the full-time course are: Darlington College of Technology, Harlow College (Journalism Division), Highbury College of Technology (Portsmouth), Lancashire Polytechnic, Richmond College (Sheffield), South Glamorgan Institute of Higher Education. Those offering the postgraduate course are: University College Cardiff

(Centre for Journalism), City University, South Glamorgan Institute of Higher Education.

There are three ways of training. The traditional way is for entrants to persuade a provincial editor to give them a six-month trial and then indenture them for three years (two-and-a half years if they have A levels, or equivalent, two years if they have a degree), during which time they are trained on and off the job. Off-the-job training and further education are undertaken in colleges and company training centres. School-leaver trainees spend two periods of block release in college, adult trainees one.

The second way is to join a one-year full-time pre-entry course run by the NCTJ, followed by indenture (three years in Scotland, one year, nine months for graduates). Minimum educational qualifications for these courses are two A levels (or equivalent) including English and two O levels (or equivalent).

Direct entrants need to have at least five O levels in grades A, B or C (or equivalent) including English language. Many editors require at least one A level (or equivalent) and over half the applicants are graduates. There is no age limit, but those who enter journalism over the age of 30 are in the minority. The NCTJ has approved certain freesheets for admittance to the newspaper training scheme. If you are thinking of applying to a freesheet, check that its trainees will be accepted for registration by the NCTJ. During indenture trainees take the Proficiency Test, the recognised professional examination. There are NCTJ-recognised in-house training schemes offered by six regional newspaper groups: the Croydon Advertiser Group, Thomson Regional Newspapers, Express and Star, Wolverhampton, Westminster Press Ltd, Kent and Sussex Courier, Eastern Counties Newspapers Ltd.

Entrants over the age of 24 are not obliged to enter into a contract of indenture, but must follow an agreed training programme to achieve Proficiency Certificate standards.

The Newspaper Society, which is the employers' association representing the regional and local press in England and Wales, and a constituent body of the NCTJ, has assumed responsibility for providing careers advice.

Periodicals

There are no indentures and periodical journalism is open to all who can get a job. There is a regulated training scheme supervised by the Periodicals Training Council (PTC) under the auspices of the Periodical Publishers Association. Trainees are given a logbook which lists the skills to be learned and this is signed by the employer section by section as they complete each part of the training. Trainees can take their logbook with them when they transfer to another employer. When the logbook is full the PTC issues a Certificate of Training.

Radio and Television
Radio and television companies frequently recruit experienced newspaper journalists. There are, however, a few trainee schemes for which there is intense competition. BBC schemes: the News Trainee Scheme begins in October and April; applicants are normally aged between 21 and 25, hold a good degree, and can show specimens of their work; the Local Radio Trainee Reporter Scheme starts in September and lasts 20 months; applicants are normally aged between 20 and 30 with educational qualifications of at least A level (or equivalent) standard. The latter scheme is not open to those who have already had formal journalistic training. Independent Television News (ITN) occasionally takes a small number of graduates with no professional experience and trains them on its Graduate Editorial Trainee Scheme. Independent Television Companies Association runs a 13-week training programme for trainee company employees who have no experience of journalism and for newspaper or radio journalists who need to learn television work. It is also suitable for journalists who have attended postgraduate courses in journalism or NCTJ courses. The Association of Independent Radio Contractors (AIRC) and the NUJ set up the Joint Advisory Committee for Radio Journalism Training which issued guidelines for colleges on the basic minimum requirements to be met by postgraduate diploma courses in radio journalism.

Courses and Awards

CNAA Degrees and Diplomas
BA Communication studies, Glasgow CT, Queen Margaret C Edinburgh
BA/BA Hons Communication studies, Trent Poly, Birmingham Poly, Coventry (Lanchester) Poly, Sheffield City Poly, Poly of Wales
BA Hons Media production, Newcastle Poly
BA Hons Media studies, Central London Poly
Diploma radio journalism, Cornwall CF&HE

CAREERS IN THE MEDIA

University Degrees
BSc/BSc Hons (Collegiate) with Public media and another subject, Leeds

Combined Subjects Degrees
Communication studies option, London Goldsmiths' C, Middlesex Poly
Communication and cultural studies option, Bristol Poly, Trinity & All Saints C Leeds
NCTJ one-year pre-entry course in newspaper journalism, Harlow C, Darlington CT, Lancashire Poly, Highbury CT Portsmouth, Richmond C Sheffield, Belfast CBS, South Glamorgan IHE
NCTJ direct-entry indentured training in newspaper journalism, Harlow C, Highbury CT, Richmond C Sheffield, South Glamorgan IHE
NCTJ proficiency test in newspaper journalism, Lancashire Poly, South Glamorgan IHE, Cornwall CF&HE
Periodical Training Trust one-year pre-entry course in periodical journalism, London C of Printing

BTEC HND
Business and finance, communication specialism, Newcastle Poly
Business and finance, journalism specialism, London C of Printing

SCOTVEC HND
Journalism studies, Napier Poly
City and Guilds 779 Media techniques (journalism and radio)

College Awards
Diploma in communication studies, Norwich City CF&HE
Graduate diploma in communication studies, Birmingham Poly
Diploma in creative communication studies, Southampton IHE
Diploma in media studies, Shirecliffe C Sheffield, South Glamorgan IHE
International diploma in journalism, Darlington CT
Diploma in radio journalism, Highbury CT Portsmouth
Certificate in fashion writing, London C of Fashion

College-based Courses
Journalism with GCE studies, Percival Whitley CFE Halifax
Periodical journalism for graduates, London C of Printing
Radio journalism, Darlington CT
Journalism and media studies, de Haviland C

JOURNALISM

Pre-entry journalism, East Surrey C
Media studies (journalism and radio), Newbury CFE, Chippenham TC

Further Information

Always send a self-addressed stamped envelope.

Association of Independent Radio Contractors, 159-169 Old Marylebone Road, London NW1 5RA
BBC Appointments, 5 Portland Place, London W1A 1AA
Independent Broadcasting Authority, 70 Brompton Road, London SW3 1EY
Independent Television Companies Association Ltd, Knighton House, 56 Mortimer Street, London W1N 8AN
Institute of Journalists, Bedford Chambers, Covent Garden, London WC2E 8HA
Joint Advisory Committee for the Training of Radio Journalists, c/o NUJ (see below)
National Council for the Training of Journalists, Carlton House, Hemnall Street, Epping, Essex CM16 4NL
National Union of Journalists, Acorn House 314 Gray's Inn Road, London WC1X 8DP
The Newspaper Society, Bloomsbury House, Bloomsbury Square, 74-77 Great Russell Street, London WC1B 3DA
Periodical Publishers Association, Imperial House, 16-19 Kingsway, London WC2 6UN
Periodical Training Council (as above)
Scottish Newspaper Proprietors' Association, Edinburgh House, 3-11 North St Andrews Street, Edinburgh EH2 1JU
Society of Women Writers and Journalists, 2 St Lawrence Close, Edgware, Middlesex HA8 6RB

Artists' and Writers' Yearbook (A & C Black)
Benn's UK Media Directory
Careers in Journalism (Kogan Page)
Careers in Television and Radio (Kogan Page)
'Financial journalism' in *How to Get a Highly Paid Job in the City* (Kogan Page)
Willing's Press Guide
Working on a Newspaper (Wayland)

Chapter 6
Publishing

Book Publishing

General (or trade) publishing is the part of the trade with which most people are familiar. It includes fiction and non-fiction, adult and children's books, whether sold in hard covers or paperback, available from shops or through book clubs.

The publishing process usually begins with a publisher or literary agent having an idea for a book. A suitable author is then found and commissioned to write it. Alternatively, an agent may have a manuscript with high sales potential for which he/she will organise an auction and then make a deal with the publisher whose offer is most favourable. Once a manuscript has been accepted, the publisher is responsible for transforming it into a book, and this will generally be done in consultation with the author. Except in the field of fiction, unsolicited manuscripts – those sent unrequested – form a very small part of publishers' output.

Usually a hardback edition comes first. Hard binding is used for books which need to last, eg library copies, reference books, sometimes class sets of textbooks. Jackets are designed and produced by the publisher's art department or commissioned from a freelance designer; the publicity department adds a blurb (promotional statement) about the book's contents, the author and, possibly, related titles. Jackets are sent to overseas agents to promote advance sales of the book among the trade, and the home trade representatives show copies to wholesalers and bookshops. When the book is ready, review copies are sent out.

Paperbacks account for about one-third of the publishing turnover in the UK. Sometimes the hardback and paperback editions of a book are produced by the same publisher, sometimes by two different publishers; usually the printed sheets come from the same print run. There are also mass-market paperback houses and they reset the type for their editions and announce any film or television tie-in on their covers.

Books for young children are usually produced in hardback. Most of them are short and full of colour illustrations and, since they tend to be bought by adults as presents, there is not a pressing need for an economy edition. Older children's books are usually paperbacked, many of them being classics on which royalties are no longer payable.

Book clubs buy a hardback, club edition from the originating publisher, who may manufacture for the club, or sell rights for a royalty. The club pays a lump sum in advance if it is a royalty-based deal; the author receives an agreed share of the net receipts from the club deal.

Overseas publishers are shown the book at some stage of production – manuscript, proof or finished copy. They may decide to buy translation rights or English language rights. The author receives an agreed percentage of such payments.

Heavily illustrated works are costly to produce and if a publisher can produce an enticing manuscript backed up by a well-illustrated dummy of the book, he/she will persuade a consortium of overseas publishers to undertake simultaneous editions, thus greatly reducing the production costs. There are companies known as packagers, which do not themselves publish but specialise in originating and producing *co-editions* to sell to publishers who may lack the resources to undertake such ambitious projects.

Specialist Publishing

Educational publishers provide the entire range from first school readers to postgraduate studies. Prices must be kept low and publishers strive to secure adoptions, ie to ensure that their titles get on to the lists of set books or recommended reading. A successful textbook brings rewards for both publisher and author over many years. Books for university studies in such subjects as history may command respectable sales to the general public.

Dictionaries, encyclopaedias and reference books require considerable investment by publishers: each requires a general editor as well as a team of sub editors, researchers and other contributors, eg picture researchers. The editorial workload is immense and must be executed to a strict deadline. Yearbooks and directories are compiled in house from information sources and answers to mailed questionnaires; they are produced under great pressure, as their commercial success is dependent upon the speed and accuracy of their updating. Computers have simplified the storage of data and reduced the work of information retrieval and updating. Encyclopaedias or extended studies (on subjects such as World War I or the twentieth century) may be produced in heavily illustrated magazine-format instalments, known as partworks, for monthly or weekly purchase from newsagents. The high cost of the complete work may not be apparent when each part is sold at a comparatively modest price. If the number of subscribers falls off, the publisher's costs will rise as the book has to be completed. At a later date, suitable extracts may be collected and republished as a hardback book.

Fine art books contain high-quality reproductions of works of art; many of them are of the works of contemporary artists. By limiting such editions to a stated number, the publisher can enhance their value. Each plate may be a very fine print and sometimes a signed print will be incorporated in each copy. These books may be sponsored by the gallery of the artist concerned.

Fine bindings are usually provided only for limited editions and in the trade fine bindings are applied only to individual orders.

Jobs in Book Publishing

Publishing houses differ in their structure, but most have three main departments: editorial, production/design, and sales/marketing. Additionally, there are the service departments found in most commercial offices: accounts, reception, personnel, warehousing and distribution. Secretaries are attached to each department; they can learn the publishing job and then move across the floor into the publishing sector.

Editorial
This is the department which attracts the most applicants, although editors are a very small percentage of the total publishing labour force. The editorial department takes the author's manuscript and, in due course, hands back a bound book; it is the department which has the most contact with the author. Editors liaise with those involved in the design, planning and production of each book, may commission illustrations and an index. They read and edit the manuscript, prepare it for the typesetter, check the proofs and are responsible for assembling all the various parts, paginated in correct order, for the printer.

The editorial director has the top position and a seat on the board. In some houses there are managing editors, who combine the roles of manager and editor. They may run a centralised copy-editing department, and commission and supervise freelance editorial workers.

Acquisitions or commissioning editors (also known as sponsoring editors or publishers) are the list builders and their main task is to find authors and books of quality. They will not necessarily have worked their way up through the department but could have been engaged because of their specialist knowledge or contacts. They must be on the alert for sales possibilities and ways to expand the market. They will be involved in buying various rights, commissioning translations, finding new authors, keeping established authors happy, negotiating with literary agents. They originate large projects and set up a team to carry them through. They must read widely and be aware of buying trends. In liaison with other departments, the editors take the accepted manuscript through the various stages to deliver a bound book within a given time at an agreed price. They read and report on commissioned and unsolicited manuscripts and proposals. They work with the minimum of supervision, drafting contracts and agreements, accepting and rejecting manuscripts, passing page proofs for production, drafting and/or approving jacket copy, catalogue copy and advance information sheets and making presentations of their books to sales representatives. They must meet their deadlines, keep within their budgets and cope with considerable stress.

Desk editors (also known as sub editors or copy editors), responsible to and supervised by a senior, read a manuscript several times, check it for copyright material and prepare it for the printer. They check references and facts, correct grammar, spelling and punctuation, discuss with, or suggest to, the author revisions, picture content, design and production schedules; choose the illustrations, and draft jacket blurb and catalogue copy. They hand the edited manuscript to the design department for production. Once the manuscript has been set in type, they send a set of proofs to the author, proof read one themselves, collate the two sets of corrections and return the proofs (via the production department) to the printer. Books with complicated make-up usually go through several proofing stages.

Desk editors may also be responsible for compiling or updating entries for directories and encyclopaedias from data supplied. Desk editors in a small company have contact with other departments, those in large companies may rarely move outside their own domain.

Editorial assistants are the beginners; most of them have secretarial skills. Under the guidance of a senior, they perform such tasks as preparing captions for illustrations, researching bibliographical information, updating books for new editions, obtaining pictures, and so on.

Paperback and book club editors whose companies buy rights in the finished product of a hardback publisher are involved in evaluating the suitability of works for their company's list. When the originating publisher first submits a work in manuscript they make suggestions about possible changes to the text, design or cover which would make it more acceptable and negotiate a contract. The editorial departments of paperback houses which originate their own titles and produce their own editions of bought-in books work on orthodox lines. A book club wishing to originate a work will generally come to an arrangement for a packaging publisher to undertake the editorial work.

Copyright and Permissions Work
A company with a long back list employs a full-time copyright and permissions editor who deals with requests from individuals and other publishers to reproduce passages or illustrations from its copyright works.

Personal Qualities
Editors need good general knowledge and an in-depth knowledge of their own field. They must be able to appreciate good writing, have a sound command of written English, a retentive memory, legible handwriting and a methodical approach to their work. A desk editor should be dedicated, accurate and able to work through constant interruptions. A commissioning editor needs imagination and a nose for what will sell.

Career Development
There is no automatic promotion ladder or salary structure. In a small company there may be no room for promotion and if you want to move up you may have to move out.

Entry Requirements and Training
A degree is useful (essential in specialist academic fields), but often insufficient by itself. There is little or no formal training; most of the work is learnt on the job. Languages are useful, as publishing is an international business, and all editors should be able to type.

Picture Research
This is a very professional wing of an editorial department and one that tends to be dominated by women. Picture researchers are provided with a list of pictures or subjects which are needed for a book, or given a copy of the manuscript, briefed on format and design and asked to provide an agreed number of suitable pictures. Some months may be allocated for the acquisition of illustrations so researchers are usually able to work on a subject in depth. Deadlines on partworks and periodicals tend to be short. Publishing houses build up their own picture archives with which picture researchers must become familiar; they also need a knowledge of worldwide sources and of copyright regulations.

Personal Qualities

Picture researchers need curiosity, tenacity, imagination, visual awareness and versatility. They must be punctilious about details and good at dealing with people as negotiation and persuasion form a large part of the job.

Entry Requirements and Training

People enter picture research with qualifications ranging from O levels (or equivalent) to a degree. Any expert knowledge is useful since pictures are required for all subjects. There is no formal pre-entry training and the work is usually learnt on the job. Experience in a library, gallery, museum or picture library would be very useful. (See also **Researcher**, p 24.)

Production

The production department is responsible for the manufacture of the books and must ensure that they are produced to the highest possible standard for the agreed price.

Production Controller

When a manuscript is delivered a word count is made, the production controller draws up an accurate specification for the book and invites tenders from typesetters, printers, paper suppliers, and binders. When all the estimates have been received, the production controller places orders for typesetting, printing and binding, purchases paper and binding materials and ensures that all the production stages (both in and outside the house) are carried out to the required standard and on schedule. When manufacture is carried out abroad, the production controller deals with foreign suppliers, freight forwarders and shippers.

Production Director (or Manager)

Production directors, who at some stage of their career will have been production controllers, have a seat on the board of directors; they are policy makers and carry considerable financial responsibility.

Production Assistant

This title is often given to someone who has entered publishing as a trainee, secretary, designer or stock controller and decides to train for production at evening or day-release classes while doing fairly undemanding production work on, for example, leaflets or reprints.

CAREERS IN THE MEDIA

Book Jackets and Covers
These are often the responsibility of one production executive who will probably engage a freelance designer to produce the work.

Personal Qualities
Production staff need business acumen, technical knowledge and the ability to administer and organise efficiently.

Entry Requirements and Training
Preliminary training is needed (courses are listed on p 93-5). Production staff have often come into publishing after working in the printing industry (see Chapter 7).

Designers
The work of the design department involves all aspects of book design: layout, fount (typeface), type sizes, spacing, style and arrangement of illustrations, jacket or cover. Designers prepare layouts, sketches, specimen pages and dummies and mark up manuscripts for the typesetter after they have been edited. Design managers (or directors) oversee all these activities. In addition, they discuss illustrated or complicated technical books with the author and editor, commission freelance artwork, arrange the in-house preparation of artwork and impose a visual style on the company product.

Entry Requirements and Training
Most designers have successfully completed art and design courses that have a large typographic element (see p 137-9).

Sales, Marketing and Publicity Personnel
For detailed information about the work of sales, marketing and publicity personnel, see Chapters 10 and 11. The main function of the sales department is to sell books and rights and the marketing and publicity departments prepare such sales aids as catalogues, price lists, leaflets, posters and display stands; they arrange book signings and other promotional activities and try to wring as much free publicity from the media as they can. The sales department will be run by a sales director and representatives usually specialise in educational, home, export or rights sales. Rights sales staff use the post and the telephone and do a great deal of their work in face-to-face negotiations; they receive overseas publishers, travel abroad to visit publishers and attend book fairs.

Entry Requirements
The majority of those recruited for a sales department are graduates, but anyone with a good educational background, numeracy and persuasive powers could apply for a sales post. The company will provide the initial training and this will be followed by in-service courses.

Graduates are often recruited into publicity and marketing departments straight from university. Applicants should be creative, be able to write lively and informative copy, have a talent for PR and a good telephone manner.

Periodical Publishing

Periodicals include magazines, professional, house and academic journals, newspaper colour supplements and comics. Whatever your interest there is a publication for you and this vast field – some 7500 titles published annually – offers a variety of careers.

The organisation of magazine groups differs from that of book publishing and has much in common with newspapers; the main areas of activity outside the service departments are editorial, advertisement sales, and circulation.

Editorial
Editors control the content of a periodical: they commission articles or visual material, write articles themselves, select suitable material from unsolicited contributions and prepare the whole for publication. When there is no art editor, they place illustrations in juxtaposition to the text, insert advertisements in the positions paid for, and give each edition the coherence and style expected by regular readers.

The editor must have a deep knowledge of the periodical's subject matter (the editor of an academic journal may be a world expert) and have a wide network of personal contacts.

Sub editors and editorial assistants prepare the copy under the editor's guidance, carry out research, check facts, obtain pictures, deal with correspondence and, in an autonomous office, do layout work. Many house journals, academic and college publications are produced entirely by part-time voluntary staff. Trade magazines have a small nucleus of highly proficient technical staff. Generally speaking, the less specialised the field, the greater the competition to get into it (women's magazines, for example); the more specialised the field, the greater the expertise that is required.

Entry Requirements
As with book publishing, pre-entry training is minimal (see p 86) and each publishing group or individual periodical will have its own requirements. Non-specialist applicants will be expected to have a wide range of general knowledge and all will need to be able to type.

Design
The range of work includes: cover design, typographical design, layout, design of advertisements and direct mail material, and the provision of illustrations. The art editor is responsible for the appearance of the magazine and needs a thorough knowledge of the readership.

Entry Requirements and Training
Designers straight from art college, or college-leavers with technical drawing ability, will need graphic training for serious work on periodicals. School-leavers who are neat workers can sometimes start work as paste-up artists (with periodical or book publishers) and train seriously once in employment. For details on training, see p 140.

Production
Production staff are trained in the printing trade. It is their responsibility to see that the magazine is available at point of sale on publication day and this involves meticulous planning and the work can be extremely stressful.

Advertisement Sales
Commercial magazines depend on advertising revenue for survival. Graduates are often recruited straight from university to sales posts and they are trained on the job.

Sales staff must know the magazine's readership and build up advantageous contacts with potential advertisers. They spend much time on research, analysis and planning, and need a persuasive manner and numerical skills.

Circulation
The circulation department must achieve maximum sales from the wholesale trade. The distribution manager is responsible for ensuring prompt delivery to wholesalers and is adept at solving transport problems. There is a team of sales representatives, each working within his/her own territory.

Personal Qualities
Sales and marketing staff must be persuasive, enthusiastic, extrovert and determined to succeed.

Entry Requirements and Training
The large magazine groups recruit graduates or people aged 21-24 who have good A levels (or equivalent). Training is given by the company.

Allied Occupations and Freelance Opportunities

The work of literary agents and scouts is described in Chapter 16, pp 155-6.

Publicist
Publicists will undertake anything from a single promotion to a complete publicity campaign. They design, plan and arrange for the printing of leaflets and catalogues, organise advertising, direct mailings, review copy distribution and press cuttings, arrange authors' tours, presentations and interviews, and some will undertake print buying, sales and marketing. Companies are usually small and entry is usually by recommendation.

Editorial, Literary and Production Services
There are companies offering the entire range of publishing services to publishers, advertisers, and public relations officers who need material to be written, prepared for press, researched, revised or updated. They recruit from experienced publishers by recommendation.

Indexing
Publisher's contracts usually call on the author either to provide his/her own index, or to pay for the cost of one provided by the publisher. Most indexers gain their initial experience in publishing house editorial departments and then work freelance.

Indexing can be taken as part of a librarianship course, the Rapid Results College offers a correspondence course, recommended by the Society of Indexers, and there are book indexing postal tutorials. The Society issues an annual Register of Indexers which it sends to all publishers.

Translation
(See Chapter 8, p 107)

Freelance Editorial Work
Readers are commissioned to report on manuscripts, proposals or foreign books which are being considered for publication. They are generally people with publishing knowledge who are expected to know of rival publications which might affect a proposed book's chances of success, or are specialists in the field concerned.

Rewriting, *copy editing* and *proof reading* are often carried out by freelances.

The arrival of the word processor has meant that there is no longer always a clear distinction between *manuscript typing* and *typesetting*. Traditional typing, commisioned by an author or publisher, is usually done by freelances, who nowadays are expected to have an electric or electronic typewriter. Typesetting can be undertaken by trained freelances who have their own equipment, but many authors now deliver a word processor disk of their manuscript, obviating the need for typesetting.

Lexicography is the preparation of definitions for dictionaries or reference books. Lexicographers usually start in house, working under the direction of an editor, and then become freelance.

Entries for encyclopaedias and yearbooks are usually compiled by *freelance writers* with specialist knowledge.

Most illustrations are produced by freelance *artists* (see Chapter 12). There is a constant demand for cover and jacket designs, as well as for the design of all printed matter used by publishing houses, design companies, advertising firms and companies wanting their own promotional material. During the summer, when publishers are preparing for the Frankfurt Book Fair, art departments work at full stretch and will sometimes take on art students during the vacation to do paste-up and layout work.

Freelance *sales representatives* may travel in a certain area for a group of small companies each too small to keep its own sales personnel on the road.

Many *picture researchers* work freelance. See p 86.

Starting Salaries

Editorial assistants £5000–£7000, commissioning editors £9000–£10,000;

PUBLISHING

picture researchers £5500; qualified production staff £7000; art department staff £6000; sales, marketing and publicity staff £7000; sales representatives £7000–£10,000 plus car.

Course and Awards

University First Degrees
BSc (Hons) Paper sciences, Manchester
BA (Hons) Typography and Graphic Communication, Reading

CNAA Polytechnic Degrees
BA Publishing, Napier
BA/BA (Hons), BSc/BSc (Hons), BEd (Hons) Publishing, Oxford

Higher Degrees awarded by Universities
MA and MA (Collegiate) Bibliography, publishing and textual studies, Leeds
MA (RCA) Printmaking, London, Royal CA
MA, MSc, MTech, MLS Publishing, Loughborough
MSc (Faculty of Science) Paper science, Manchester
MPhil Publishing studies, Stirling

Higher Degrees awarded by Polytechnics
MA Printmaking, Brighton

Diplomas awarded by Polytechnics
Postgraduate Diploma, Printmaking, Brighton
BTEC/HND Printing, Manchester
BTEC/HND Printing, Trent

Certificates awarded by Polytechnics
BTEC/HND Printing; Polytechnic Certificate Printing; Printing and photographic technology, Manchester.

National Diploma
BTEC HND Printing and publishing specialism, London C of Printing

College Diplomas
Diploma in publishing and book production, Exeter CA&T

Diploma in publishing production; Diploma in printing and publishing studies for graduates, London C of Printing

Pre-entry Training
Training has always been available (and essential) for production and design staff; nowadays jobs are difficult to obtain without it.
 The London College of Printing offers the following courses:
Diploma in printing and publishing for graduates (17 weeks, full-time)
Diploma course in book and periodical production (one-year, full-time) for those currently engaged in book or periodical publishing or wishing to prepare for such employment.
Diploma course in photolithography (one-year, full-time)
BTEC National diploma in business studies: (two-year, full-time) for those intending to take up administrative positions in book, magazine and newspaper publishing
BTEC HND in business studies: (two-year, full-time) for those intending to take up postitions in publishing.
 The Oxford Polytechnic offers the following courses:
A publishing degree course, part of its modular course, which gives students the opportunity to study contemporary publishing, as a medium and as a practice, from many different perspectives (one-year full-time or seven-year part-time) (see above). Diploma in advanced studies in publishing, a vocational course of particular interest to graduates or those already in post (one-year full-time, eight-term part-time)

In-service Courses
The Publishers Group Training Service, Beards House, Acrelands Green, Pleshey, Essex runs two-day courses in central London on a variety of publishing subjects.
 The London College of Printing offers formal courses: a three-week full-time intensive course and one- or two-year evening certificate courses; enquiries to Mr LJ Robinson, London College of Printing, Back Hill, Clerkenwell, London EC1R 5EN.
 Book House Training Centre (BHTC), 45 East Hill, Wandsworth, London SW18 2QZ is the non-statutory training organisation for publishing and book selling. It runs foundation, editorial, category publishing, publishing and the law, production, marketing and management courses, details of which are obtainable from the BHTC.

Informal Learning
The following groups offer informal meetings, seminars and

conferences, details of which are advertised, either to members only, or to the trade as a whole, via the *Bookseller*:
The British Association of Industrial Editors, 3 Locks Yard, High Street, Sevenoaks, Kent TN13 1LT
IBIS Information Services Ltd, Waterside, Lowbell Lane, London Colney, St Albans, Hertfordshire AL2 1DX.

Professional Institutions, Associations, Awards

London School of Publishing, 47 Red Lion Street, London WC1R 4PF was formed to provide training courses for people wishing to gain qualifications to work or advance their careers in publishing and awards a Diploma
The Society of Indexers, Seagulls, 16 Green Road, Birchington, Kent CT7 9JZ
Society of Picture Researchers and Editors, BM Box 259, London WC1N 3XX

Further Information

Careers in Publishing (Kogan Page)
Working in Books (COIC)

Chapter 7
Printing

Printing is one of Britain's largest industries and the British printing industry is one of the largest in Europe. The products of the industry are extremely varied and include books, magazines, newspapers, maps, packaging (made of paper, carton, plastic and glass), bank notes, credit cards, floor and wall coverings. There are a number of different processes, each appropriate for certain end products. Only those kinds of work which might be of interest to someone wanting to work in the media are outlined in this chapter.

Typesetting

Before any printing job is undertaken, customer and printer discuss such questions as design, typeface, format and layout. If the customer is, say, a book publisher the design work will probably be done by the publishing-house designer. In a large printing firm there will be an in-house designer to advise customers who do not have their own designer. In a small firm the typesetter, working with a keyboard and visual display unit (VDU), will do design work. Very few printers still set type by hand only, though many still use machines that set fresh type in hot metal for each job. Today, virtually all text is set by a machine operator using a computer keyboard, laid out like a QWERTY typewriter, and a VDU. With the latest equipment much of the make-up into pages can be controlled by the keyboard operator. The text comes out on film or paper, coded tape or magnetic disk, or laser and the keyboard operator produces a proof. In a large firm there will be a reader who checks the text for errors; nowadays, however, many firms pass most of the responsibility for proofreading to their clients.

Typesetting may be part of a whole printing operation or may be a service which is sold to a client, eg an advertising agent or designer. When type is being set for an item which is reprinted regularly, eg a directory, the text will be stored in disk or tape.

Good operators have excellent speeds and are very accurate. The work calls for concentration and can cause eye-strain. It is possible to move from typesetting into design.

Reproduction

Nowadays, the reproduction of colour pictures is generally carried out on electronic scanners, which have largely replaced cameras in the production of colour separations and have also reduced the role of film retouchers. Camera operators photograph the original of a drawing or photograph and from this produce a negative or positive as required. In colour work a separate piece of film for each colour has to be produced. The camera operator needs considerable skill and experience; much less skill is needed to work an electronic scanner.

Retouching

After film has been produced, the retoucher removes blemishes and adjusts colour tones. Much of the work can now be done by electronic scanner, but there are still areas where it has to be done by hand.

Page Make-up/Paste-up Work

Paste-up artists trim copy and illustrations to the required size and paste them up into the final page layout, which is photographed so that plates can be made. This work is called for less and less because page make-up is now done on a VDU.

Machine Printing

The only person in the trade who is entitled to be called a printer is the machine minder. The size of a machine's crew will depend upon the size of the press and on the agreement negotiated between employers and unions. A small press may need only one minder, whereas a large four-colour offset litho press may have two minders and two assistants. Minder and crew set up and run the press for each job and it is their responsibility to ensure that the printing is accurate and consistent throughout the run.

Binding and Finishing

The services included under this heading can be anything from simply trimming sheets on a guillotine to full-scale leather binding.

Office Work

In a large printing works there are office jobs for estimators, costing clerks and sales staff; small independent printers do all these jobs themselves.

The Work Printers Do

Jobbing
Most people's idea of a printer is the jobbing printer, usually a small firm that prints a wide variety of things from visiting cards to colour brochures. Jobbing printers usually have a range of equipment and employees with different skills – typesetters, scanner operators, machine minders and finishers. Presses not only use different processes, they also come in a great many sizes from the very small used for printing, eg letterheads, to the huge four-colour machine that can print maps and wall-charts.

Book and Magazine Printing
Books represent approximately 10 per cent of the output and employment of the printing industry in the UK and the book-printing section of the industry is the one that has been most affected by competition from abroad. Book production can be spread over several months. Magazines, on the other hand, often have to be ready in a matter of days or hours and for this reason magazine typesetters may have to work in shifts. Magazine printers normally have all the finishing machinery needed to complete the job and may have automatic enveloping or wrapping machines.

Newspapers
The national newspapers have their own presses, but provincial or local papers are sometimes printed by firms that also do commercial work. Jobs in the press are roughly similar to those in the printing industry, but

staff are normally recruited from among fully trained printers in the industry at large.

Job Opportunities

It is true that more and more processes in printing will be automated; however, there will be a continuing need for supervisors and managers, technicians, production workers, and semi-skilled operatives, but less demand for those with traditional craft-based training. Overall, there will be fewer jobs but very exciting opportunities for those willing to seize them. There is no formal career structure and anyone entering the industry must be flexible, ready to retrain and to change jobs.

Although it is true that neither unions nor employers oppose the employment of women in any branch of the industry, this relatively new attitude to equal opportunities has coincided with a general downturn in recruitment. Various technical changes have made the industry more 'suitable' for women. There now remains little of the heavy work associated with hot-metal typesetting and today the weight of a page is simply the weight of a piece of paper. Furthermore, many of the skills now required are more likely to be possessed by women than men; for example, women are often faster and more accurate keyboard operators (and are likely to learn typing at school) and fewer women than men have defects in colour vision, though most aspects of colour printing have remained a male preserve.

Starting Salaries

Starting salaries vary but average minimum weekly figures for those aged 16–18 are £68–£90 for compositors, keyboard operators, machine assistants, finishers and binders. An experienced machine assistant doing six-colour work averages £125 per week.

Personal Qualities

In many sections of the printing industry it is essential to have perfect colour vision. Keyboard operators and typesetters must have a sound knowledge of English (particularly of spelling and punctuation). Operatives are always expected to have good keyboard speeds but it is even more important for them to be accurate. They need spatial awareness and should have a flair for design. Machine minders need a grounding in electronics as much of the machinery is computer controlled. This very high-precision work calls for great concentration and constant attention to detail. For binding and finishing work good machine skills are needed.

Entry Requirements and Training

Academic qualifications are not mandatory for craft workers but the British Printing Industries Federation (BPIF) states that the following minimum qualifications are preferred. For typesetters, keyboard operators, photosetters, readers, make-up artists and binders: CSE grade 2 (or equivalent) passes in English, maths, art and handicraft; for machine minders and finishers, maths, English, technical drawing and a science. For office work people with qualifications ranging from O levels (or equivalent) to a degree are recruited. Individual firms have their own recruitment policy and stipulate the qualifications they require applicants to hold.

Trainees under the age of 18 follow a two-way unit-based training scheme and are given leave of absence to attend courses. Training for those over the age of 18 is at the discretion of the individual employer.

Courses and Awards

University First Degrees
BSc Hons Paper science, Manchester
BA Hons Typography and graphic communication, Reading

CNAA Polytechnic Degrees
BSc/BSc Hons Printing and packaging technology, Hatfield

University Higher Degrees
MSc Paper science, Manchester
MA Printmaking, Royal C of Art

Polytechnic Higher Degrees
MA Printmaking, Brighton

PRINTING

Diplomas and Certificates awarded by Polytechnics
Postgraduate diploma, Printmaking, Brighton
BTEC HND, Printing Manchester
BTEC HND, Printing, Trent
BTEC HND, HNC Printing, Polytechnic certificate printing, Printing and photographic technology, Manchester

National Certificates and Diplomas
BTEC HND in Business and finance (Printing and publishing specialism)
BTEC (Board for Design) NC in Design for print, NC in Graphics and production, NC in Printing, NC in Design (Printing and graphic production), NC in Printing (Small offset techniques), ND in Design (Print and design production), ND in Design (Printing), ND in Design (Reprography), ND in Design (Typographical design), HNC Craft Bookbinding (Design and production), HNC in Printing, HNC in Typographical design, HND in Printing, HND in Photographic technology, HND in Typographic design
SCOTVEC NC Modules, Printing, Printing (administration), Printing (technical production)
SCOTVEC HNC in printing, in printing inks, in paper technology
SCOTVEC HND in printing (administration and production)

City and Guilds
063 Printing ink, 500 Paper and board making I and II, 501 Printing machine operatives, 509 Flexographic printing, 515 Screen process printing, 517 Reprographic techniques, 518 Printing (various options), 521 Bookbinding and Advanced certificate in bookbinding, 523 Printing (combined modules and various options), 530 Introduction to management (graphic communication industries), 532 Design for printing, 534 Printing production management, 536 Communication of technical information

College Awards
The London College of Printing runs courses leading to certificates in printing techniques, craft bookbinding, advanced typographic design and to diplomas in graphic origination and reproduction, printing and publishing studies for graduates, reprographic techniques.
Certificate in craft bookbinding and Advanced certificate, London C of Printing
Certificate in design for print, Barnfield C, Luton CHE, Redditch C

Certificate in Pre-printing processes (Origination and production, London C of Printing)
Certificate in printed communication, South Glamorgan IHE
Certificate in printing and the graphic arts, Brighton Poly
Certificate in printing and photographic technology Manchester Poly
Certificate in printing techniques, London C of Printing, Liverpool CFE, Berkshire CA&D
Certificate in reprographic technical management, Watford C
Higher certificate in typographic design, Watford C
Small offset lithographic certificate, Cleveland CA&D
Diploma in creative screen printing, London C of Printing
Diploma in design for printing, Central Liverpool CFE, Glasgow CB&P
Diploma in graphic origination and reproduction, London C of Printing
Diploma in graphic reproduction, Watford C, Glasgow CB&P
Diploma in lithography, Watford C
Diploma in printing studies for graduates, London C of Printing
Diploma in printing, Kitson CT, Leeds
Diploma in printing administration, Glasgow
Diploma in reprographic techniques, London C of Printing

College-based Courses
Advanced techniques in letter assembly systems, Manchester Poly
Bookbinding and book conservation, Matthew Boulton TC, Birmingham
Printing workshop experience, Liverpool CFE
Computer controlled phototypesetting, Cambridgeshire CA&T
Foundation course in printing, Colchester I, Berkshire CA&D, Wearside CFE
Foundation course in printing and reprography, Barking CT
Foundation course in graphic communication and printing, Matthew Boulton TC
Graphic communication media, South Fields CFE, Leicester
Graphic reproduction, Cambridgeshire CA&T
Photocomposition and printing design, Cambridgeshire CA&T
Printing administration, Ulster
Reprographic course for the in-plant and small offset user, Cambridgeshire CA&T

Professional Institutions, Associations and Awards

The British Printing Industries Federation (BPIF), 11 Bedford Row, London WC1R 4DX awards certificates in Printing administration, Estimating, Printing office procedure, Advanced costing, Advanced offset lithography estimating, and has a course, Introduction to printing technology, which can be taken at CF/HE throughout the UK.

British Printing Society, 96 Sparrows Herne, Basildon, Essex SS16 5EX

The Institute of Printing, 8 Lonsdale Gardens, Tunbridge Wells, Kent TN1 1NU has the following categories of membership: Fellow, Honorary Fellow, Member, Graduate, Affiliate and Student.

The Institute of Reprographic Technology, St Catherines, 186 Denmark Road, Lowestoft, Suffolk NR32 2EN arranges lectures, demonstrations, educational visits and conferences and holds examinations leading to its certificate and diploma. There are five categories of membership: Student, Affiliate, Associate, Member, Fellow.

Society of Typographical Designers, Wellington House, Church Road, Ashford, Kent TN14 1PE

Further Information

Careers in Printing (Kogan Page)
How to Become a Printing Apprentice (BPIF)

Chapter 8
Writing

'I enjoy writing, I'm quite good at it, and I'd like a career in the media. What should I do?'

If your long-term aim is to become a full-time freelance writer you should probably start by looking for a salaried job, because you will need a regular income while you are building up your reputation and your contacts and finding out what the openings are. You may have gained an arts degree and then gone into some totally unrelated field such as merchant banking or marketing and are doing your writing in the evenings and at weekends. It requires great strength of mind to make yourself sit down and write at the end of a hard day and only the most dedicated complete anything under these circumstances, but it can be done and the satisfaction of having something accepted keeps you at it.

You may, on the other hand, have gone straight into a 'writing' job and become a trainee reporter, copywriter, public relations officer or joined an editorial department in a publishing house. Possibly an interesting career in one of these fields will open up to you, but if it does not you will have served a useful apprenticeship and learnt how to turn out a given number of words on a given subject to a deadline. There are chapters on journalism (5), advertising (9), public relations (10) and publishing (6).

Many people who start out as salaried employees in an advertising agency, PR consultancy or publishing house go freelance after a few years and gradually widen the scope of their writing as they discover where their interests and talents lie. There are any number of potential markets for work of all sorts; only a very small proportion of published writing is uncommissioned so what you need to do is learn where the markets are, how to exploit them and plan your schedule so that you have regular payments coming in. A writer, like an investor, should build up a portfolio of short- and long-term projects, one-off assignments and regular earners; you can obtain advice on how to do this from the Writer's Portfolio Service 51 Washington Road, Maldon, Essex CM9 6BN. You should also look into the question of getting a literary agent (see pp 155-6) to market your work for you as you can waste a great deal of time waiting to hear from publishers to whom you have sent an unsolicited (and possibly unsuitable) manuscript. Literary agents are listed in the *Writers' and Artists' Yearbook* (A & C Black).

The Markets

Magazines and newspapers offer the biggest potential market to the freelance writer. There are some 7500 periodicals published in the UK: special and general interest publications, consumer and business magazines, learned journals, house magazines and publications targeted on certain age groups. Before you submit any material, study the market carefully; read several issues of the publication you are thinking of approaching and try to get an idea of its style and readership etc. The *Writers' and Artists' Yearbook* lists English language newspapers and magazines and provides information about the kind of material they seek, their rates of pay etc. Other useful reference works are *The Writer's Handbook*, *Willing's Press Guide*, *Benn's Media Directory*, *Freelance Writing and Photography* and *Contributor's Bulletin*.

Newspapers fall into the following categories: national, regional and local (the last category includes freesheets) and all accept contributions from freelances. A good starting point is the local press though the demand is generally for short pieces and rates of pay are low. You could send in regular miscellaneous feature articles or become a special contributor on a subject, eg motoring or DIY, of which you have special knowledge.

Fiction is a difficult market to break into. It generates high earnings for the successful few but the sales of most first novels are numbered only in hundreds and publishers turn down thousands of unsolicited manuscripts every year. Romantic fiction, on the other hand, flourishes and can generate annual incomes that fall into the top tax bracket. There is a big demand for magazine stories and for novels. The major publishers of romantic novels encourage new writers and supply guidelines on plot and character. Every fiction writer hopes to earn subsidiary rights – paperback, foreign, serialisation, digest, book club and film rights – and an agent may be able to negotiate better terms for you then your original publisher.

The *non-fiction* market is more than four times the size of the fiction market and includes the lucrative educational sector. Very few unsolicited non-fiction manuscripts are published so before you start work on a non-fiction book you should interest a publisher. Write a preliminary letter and enclose a synopsis. If the publisher is at all interested, he/she will want to discuss the project with you and will very probably be able to make helpful suggestions for improvements. You should also consult the Arts Council's 'books in progress' service to find out whether anyone else is working on the same subject.

Children's books include both fiction and non-fiction and publishers usually divide the readers into three age groups: the under eights, the eights to fifteens, and young adults. Illustrations in books for younger children are as important as the text and if you can do your own you will make twice as much money, but if you cannot you will at least be consulted about the choice of artist.

Broadcasting offers enormous scope, radio more than television, and with radio there is the added attraction that you may be asked to broadcast your own material if you have a good microphone manner. Television, on the other hand, pays better. You should be thoroughly familiar with the output of the station/channel/service that you would like to contribute to and it is important to submit your material to the right department; for example, BBC radio is divided into drama, light entertainment, talks and documentaries, music, Radio 1, Radio 2, outside broadcasts and current affairs. Broadcasting organisations do not expect writers to produce only original work; sometimes they are commissioned to make adaptations of novels or short stories or to contribute episodes to a long-running serial. You will find the following publications useful: *Notes on Radio Drama* (BBC), *Writing for the BBC* (BBC), *Writing for Television* (A & C Black) and *The Way to Write for Television* (Elm Tree Books).

Feature films may start life as short stories or novels and the adaptations are often made by established writers. Script writers must think visually, understand how films are put together and be able to imagine the finished picture. If you have an idea for an original screenplay the best way to try to market it is through an agent who specialises in film scripts. Only a minute proportion of scripts are accepted for development and very few finally get made into films. The *Writers' and Artists' Yearbook* shows how to set out a screenplay manuscript. You can learn script-writing techniques at film school (see p 42) and script writing for television commercials provides good practice in visual storytelling.

It is hard when you are an unknown *playwright* to find a producer who will put on your play; it should be easier to persuade an amateur group or provincial repertory theatre to perform your work. You can discover what has been produced where by reading the *Stage* which publishes accounts of repertory theatre productions of new plays. The Arts

Council's *New Theatre Writing Scheme* outlines various forms of assistance available to playwrights and to theatres wishing to commission new plays.

Other Sources of Income

Translation can be divided into two main categories: technical, scientific commercial, eg textbooks, instruction manuals, learned articles, research findings, etc, and literary, eg novels, plays, poems etc. The former is well paid and calls for expert knowledge of the subject. There are salaried posts for translators, you can find work through a translation agency or you can build up your own clientele. Literary translation is a difficult field to break into. Publishers pay scouts (see p 156) to look out for suitable foreign books and when they buy the rights on a book they commission a translation, generally from an established translator or author or an expert in the field, eg an academic. It is not advisable to submit an unsolicited translation of a whole book to a publisher; instead, write a letter asking if you may submit an extended sample of your work. Literary translators always translate into their mother tongue, they need an excellent command of English and great awareness of style.

Ghost writers may rewrite manuscripts that were too badly written to be published in the form in which they were submitted – this work is an extended form of copy-editing – or they may originate books – usually 'autobiographies' of well-known personalities.

Getting Started

Writing is an occupation where nothing succeeds like success; that is to say, once you have satisfactorily completed your first job others will follow. The difficult part is breaking in and when the rejection slips come you just have to try again with another publisher, periodical or radio station. All good writers have been rejected and many a publisher has failed to spot a best seller. You can save yourself both time and anguish by observing a few elementary rules when presenting work. Your text should be typed double spaced on A4 paper; leave generous margins and use one side of the paper only. Send a stamped addressed envelope for the return of your manuscript (or a postal order to cover the postage of a parcel). Not all publishers will read unsolicited manuscripts so it is advisable to write an exploratory letter.

Research before you submit: how long are the articles in this periodical, does that publisher like steaming sex or happily-ever-after romance, who listens to this radio network, what sort of audience go to that theatre?

If you intend to employ an agent, consult the *Writers' and Artists' Yearbook*, which gives information on commission rates, reading fees, specialisation and whether or not a preliminary letter is needed.

Earnings

Rates of pay are nearly always laid down by the person who accepts your work and you should be clear about the size of the fee you can expect and when it will be paid (on receipt of manuscript or on publication?) before you sign a contract. The BBC, for example, has two rates – one for established and one for unknown contributors. You should find out whether you will be paid for repeat performances and/or reprints. An agent will negotiate fees for a client (and will take a percentage of the earnings). Book publishers generally pay an advance on royalties. When you are hired to provide a writing service, eg to produce the text of a training brochure, you can state your price and your fee must cover the time it takes you to write the piece, your overheads and your profit. But remember your price has to be competitive.

Training

See pp 79-81, courses for journalists.
Combined subjects degree course with writing option, Crewe and Alsager CHE
College-based writing course (American university programme, 1st year) Ithaca C, London.
There are a number of correspondence courses available, some of which offer you your money back if you do not manage to earn with your writing the cost of the course fees. Opinions are divided about the usefulness of such courses; many people claim that writing cannot be taught, though most would agree that writing courses can teach you about markets and something about the techniques of writing for a number of different media. Make thorough enquiries before you enrol for a course and read the small print.

Further Information

Always send a self-addressed stamped envelope.

The Association of Authors' Agents, 49 Blenheim Crescent, London W11 2EF
The Authors' Lending and Copyright Society Ltd, 7 Ridgmount Street, London WC1E 7AE
The Society of Authors, 84 Drayton Gardens, London SW10 9SB
The Writers' Guild of Great Britain, 430 Edgware Road, London W2 1EH
Writing for a Living (Kogan Page)

Chapter 9
Advertising

Advertisements are all around us: in newspapers and magazines, on television and the radio, in the cinema, at points of sale and they come through our letter boxes in the form of unsolicited mailshots. All these advertisements have been planned, created and their effectiveness is monitored.

Most people think of advertising as creative work, but the large and complex advertising industry needs people with a wide range of skills and there are relatively few creative staff compared with those involved in sales, marketing, buying, secretarial and clerical work.

Commercial advertising, the most familiar and very much the largest section of the industry, is the promotion of goods and services in order to stimulate demand. There is also non-commercial advertising, eg the government's AIDS-education campaign, and personal advertising, eg the placing of 'for sale' notices in the classified columns of a newspaper. The industry is tripartite, consisting of the advertisers, eg a company with a product or service to market; those who design and produce advertisements, ie the advertising agencies and freelances, film and independent production companies; and those who own advertising space and time, ie newspapers and magazines, commercial radio and television companies and hoarding companies. All have their own trade organisations which join together under the umbrella of the Advertising Association. The structure of the industry is very fluid and there is a great deal of mobility within it.

Commercial advertising includes industrial advertising, eg of agricultural machinery or pharmaceutical products, and the target groups are reached through the trade/professional press, mailshots, leaflet circulation, exhibitions, trade fairs and travelling sales personnel. Service advertising is practised by such organisations as building societies. Consumer advertising, of which we are all the targets, uses the press, radio, television, mailshots, leaflet circulation, special offer and competition promotions.

Advertising exists to inform potential customers about new products and to remind existing customers of established products. The message stays in the mind if it is memorable and frequently repeated. There are stringent codes of practice governing all kinds of advertising.

Working for an Advertiser

Most big companies, particularly those making fast-moving consumer goods, have an advertising department which will work closely with the marketing department. It is rare for a company to make its own advertising material, though some do, eg large department stores, and employ artists, copywriters and photographers. An advertising department is usually a unit of fewer than ten people whose jobs include budgeting and media planning, selecting and liaising with the company's advertising agency, discussing advertising strategy and objectives with the company's managers, and supervising the internal and external services involved in the execution of advertising plans. A few graduates are recruited each year on the 'milk round', but the most usual way to obtain a post is to write on spec to a number of suitable employers.

Working in an Agency

There are five main areas of work in an agency: account management and planning, creative work, production, traffic or control, and media planning. At the centre of operations in most agencies are the *account directors*, who have overall responsibility for a number of accounts; they meet clients to discuss the broad objectives and progress of their advertising campaigns. *Account executives* interpret a client's wishes, they co-ordinate and supervise the work of the different creative groups, seek advice from other experts such as *media executives*, and then present the ideas most likely to meet with the client's approval. They also monitor the progress of clients' and their competitors' campaigns and offer clients advice on new product development. They may carry out or commission market research. There are a number of other variations and levels within account handling, particularly in specialised fields, eg recruitment advertising.

An agency's success depends upon its creative department. This is usually run by a *creative director* supervising the work of *copywriters*, who write the texts of advertisements, *script writers*, who write radio and television commercials, *artists/designers*, *photographers*, *typographers* and *printers*. Creative work can be extremely varied, as an agency may have as many as 60 different clients, and it is done to a brief, though this will not always be specific and the creative team will be expected to contribute ideas. There are separate chapters on artists (12), designers (13), writing (8), photography (14) and printing (7).

Production department staff arrange for the advertisements to be made; they liaise with film, video and radio production companies, photographers, illustrators, typographers and printers.

The *traffic department* (sometimes called 'control') obtains clearance on television commercials, co-ordinates and logs the arrival and despatch of artwork, proofs and all the other items that move through an agency.

The planners and buyers in the *media department*, briefed as to the target audience and budget limitations, use research data on press readership and radio and television listening and viewing patterns to determine which medium to use and when and how often to use it. Media planning is largely statistical work and requires the ability to relate creative requirements to available media. Media buying is a straight commercial function and involves hard bargaining with the media owners. The job is stressful and calls for both stamina and business sense.

Working in Newspapers and Magazines

There are over 1500 newspapers in the UK and over 7000 professional, trade and technical publications and consumer magazines, most of which are only able to exist because they sell advertising space. In fact, the only source of revenue for freesheets is their advertising space. The two main types of job on the advertising side of the print media are: space selling for display or classified advertisements and marketing, ie promotion and circulation. In a large organisation the two departments are kept separate, but in a regional newspaper they are likely to be under one head.

Display space is bought by advertising agencies, commercial firms, financial institutions, retail outlets, political parties, government departments etc for promotional purposes, to advertise products and services and to make announcements of public interest. Advertising staff keep informed of forthcoming editorial features in order to plan campaigns to attract new advertisers.

Classified advertisements – 'Situations vacant', 'Situations wanted', 'For sale' etc – are placed by private individuals and by businesses. Classified sales staff do most of their work by telephone and therefore need a good telephone manner.

Working in Television and Radio

Over the last few years there has been little expansion in the advertising departments of the major independent television companies. They sell airtime on a spot basis and rates vary according to region, day of the week, time of day etc. Much television airtime is now sold direct from a video display unit and the number of sales staff, including those engaged on research and marketing services, has dropped by 20 per cent. However, as cable television spreads, there should be more jobs available. Sales executives spend much of their time selling by telephone and only the most senior go out into the field. Television and radio marketing department staff need a detailed knowledge of their audience.

Airtime on commercial radio is also sold on a spot basis. Station staff sell to local advertisers and very often prepare the commercials for them, but all stations, except Capital Radio, sell to national advertisers through Independent Radio Sales and Broadcast Marketing Services. More jobs should become available once the government's plans for radio start to be implemented. (See also pp 27-30.)

Working Freelance

Many agencies have pared down their permanent staff to the minimum and a lot of people on the creative side of advertising now work freelance. Agencies keep lists of freelance copywriters, artists/designers or photographers whose work they know and whom they contact when a suitable job comes up. It is highly desirable for a freelance to have – or have the use of – a fax.

Personal Qualities

This is work for people who are outgoing and articulate, who thrive under pressure and who are able to work well in a team. Account and media executives should be leaders and organisers; they must be persuasive, critical, enthusiastic and confident and possess considerable business acumen. In addition to their talent and expertise, creative staff must possess imagination, ingenuity and an inexhaustible fund of new ideas. They need to be self-critical, adaptable and resilient, as nine out of ten ideas end up in the wastepaper basket.

Job Opportunities

There are agencies all over the UK and their names can be found in the Yellow Pages. The very large agencies which handle international accounts are in London. Jobs are advertised in the quality press, *Campaign*, *Time Out*, *Marketing Week*, *Marketing*, and *Media Week*. The Advertising Association recommends job seekers to inform themselves of the topics of current concern in the business, new advertising campaigns and media trends by reading these publications and to write round 'selling' themselves, by means of a carefully prepared CV, to agencies and commercial firms. Before you can work freelance you will need in-house experience.

Starting Salaries

Trainees' salaries start at about £6000 but can rise rapidly if you perform well.

Career Development

Competition for jobs is keen and many people are prepared to accept a lowly office job just to get a foot in the door. Promotion comes soon to those with talent. There is a great deal of job mobility in the advertising industry; people move between agencies, set themselves up as freelances, open their own businesses or move into related work, eg public relations or marketing.

Entry Requirements and Training

There are no specific entry requirements for the advertising industry and people who entered agencies with few academic qualifications have risen to the top. Proven talent, however, is needed. Nowadays nearly all companies or agencies demand a minimum of five O levels (or equivalent), including English and mathematics, and many ask for A levels (or equivalent). There are graduate training schemes operating in both companies and agencies and usually any degree is acceptable. Art and design qualifications (see pp 133-5 and 140) are practically indispensable for those who want to work on the creative side, and if you apply for a creative post you should take samples of your work to an interview. Some agencies ask applicants to take a 'copy' test. Most training is given on the job. Courses are run by the Communication, Advertising and Marketing Education Foundation (CAM) and by the Institute of Practitioners in Advertising.

CAM is the examining body for 20 institutions and organisations representing the UK communications industries. Broadly, they cover the fields of media, marketing, advertising and public relations and the examinations reflect this. Examinations are set by examiners from the relevant industry sector concerned, together with academics who have practical experience in these areas. CAM qualifications are, therefore, industry-led. Part 1, the Certificate, covers marketing, advertising, public relations, media, sale promotion/direct marketing, research and behaviour studies. Part 2, the Diploma, concerns management and strategy, and public relations or advertising or sales promotion or direct marketing. Entry requirements for Part 1: candidates must be at least 18 and must meet one of the following criteria: they must hold any UK degree, or two A levels (or equivalent) and at least three O levels (or equivalent), one of which must be English language; or have been in full-time employment in a relevant part of the communication business for at least one year and have five O levels (or equivalent) including English language; hold a BTEC or SCOTVEC national certificate or diploma in business studies; or have passed the London Chamber of Commerce and industry third level group diploma in advertising, marketing and public relations, or the International Advertising Association basic certificate in advertising, or have successfully completed a CAM-recognised foundation course. Details of course content, methods of study and a list of colleges offering courses can be obtained from CAM.

Other Awards

International Advertising Association Basic Certificate, Greenwich C, Distributive Trades C
International Advertising Association Diploma, Distributive Trades C
BTEC HND in Business and finance, Advertising specialism, Luton CHE, Watford C, Distributive Trades C, Stockport CT, Bristol Poly
BTEC HND in Business and finance, Design for visual communication, Newcastle upon Tyne Poly
London Chamber of Commerce: Advertising (Higher), Distributive Trades C

College Awards
Certificate in advertising, Diploma in advertising, Diploma in advertising copywriting, Watford C

Professional Institutions and Associations

Advertising Association (see CAM)
Communication Advertising and Marketing Education Foundation (CAM), Abford House, 15 Wilton Road, London SW1V 1NJ
Institute of Practitioners in Advertising, 44 Belgrave Square, London SW1X 8QS

Further Information

Advertising (Association of Graduate Careers Avisory Services)
The Advertising Business, The Advertising Media, The Advertising Agency, Advertising on Television, The Regulation of Advertising, Facts and Figures on Advertising (Advertising Association)
Careers in Marketing, Advertising and Public Relations (Kogan Page)
How to Get On in Marketing, Advertising and Public Relations (Kogan Page)
The Kogan Page Guide to Careers in Arts, Crafts and Design
Working in Advertising and Public Relations (COIC)
(See also Chapters 10 on public relations and 11 on marketing.)

Chapter 10
Public Relations

Public relations (PR) is not, as some people imagine, a suspect whitewashing activity, but is the 'deliberate, planned and sustained effort to establish and maintain mutual understanding between an organisation and its public'. It is the promotion of the organisation itself and should not be confused with advertising (see Chapter 9), which is the promotion of goods and services offered for sale, though, obviously, PR that manages to project a good company image will boost sales.

In commerce and industry, PR is a top management responsibility and is generally handled in house, whereas advertising is an operational responsibility and is often handled by an agency. Furthermore, PR is a two-way process; not only does it involve disseminating information about an organisation, it also involves dealing with public reaction – which can sometimes be hostile – to the organisation and its activities and reporting to senior management. There has been a re-evaluation of PR over the past decade or so as more companies are realising that they are socially accountable. Pressure groups – articulate, organised and adept at exploiting the media – are here to stay and no organisation or institution can afford to ignore them or underestimate their power.

Private- or public-sector organisations identify a number of target groups at which to aim their PR activities. These include: potential users, who may be members of the public at large or of some select group, eg the dental profession or air travellers; shareholders, who have voting rights at AGMs; journalists in the opinion-forming media; the community in which the organisation is located and from which it draws actual or potential employees; school- and college-leavers, whom it may wish to recruit – the PR work in this instance will be done in conjunction with personnel and recruiting departments; local government, whose decisions on such matters as planning permission and rates will affect the organisation; central government and, possibly, the European Parliament; national and local pressure groups, eg environmental activists. To these can be added the organisation's own employees. It is important to foster good employee relations and one of the ways in which management and staff can communicate is through a house magazine, which will usually be produced by the PR department. Sponsorship of sport and the arts is playing an increasingly important part in corporate PR and a company that ties up large sums over longish periods, eg £100,000 over five years, will have a department working full time on projects. (See pp 151-3).

Central and local government have PR departments through which they brief ministers and officials and explain their policies to the general public and to selected target groups. The Central Office of Information is a common service agency for all government departments, preparing and distributing publicity and reference material and offering technical advice on matters relating to publicity.

The police and the armed services use PR to explain their work, improve their public image and, sometimes, to recruit. Charities, trade associations, professional bodies, trade unions, political parties all use PR to make themselves and their activities known.

PR officers must have a thorough knowledge of the media at their disposal in order to be able to use them to greatest effect. Target groups can be reached in a variety of ways: through the written word in press releases, brochures, annual reports, leaflets and house magazines; through visual material – logos, photographs, exhibitions, displays; through videos, live presentations and briefing sessions; through conference, receptions, open days and trade fairs.

In a small organisation, a PR officer can expect to oversee a wide variety of projects from brochure production to reception planning and will probably call upon specialists, eg design studios and catering firms, to do the actual work. A large organisation will produce much of its own PR material and employ a staff of people doing specialised work, eg writing press releases or making slides and film strips for lectures and conferences.

PR consultancies specialise, eg in video promotions, or offer the full range of PR services. Financial PR, which plays an important part in takeovers, mergers and the launch of new share issues, is a profitable and expanding branch of the industry and there are companies which specialise in this kind of work. Experienced journalists often move into financial PR tempted by the high salaries (in the region of £25,000 to £30,000 plus car). The City Communications Organisation acts as a clearing house for City institutions.

Personal Qualities

PR officers must be excellent communicators, but as PR is a two-way process, they must also be responsive to public reaction. They need imagination, creativity and organisational skills. Anyone wanting to enter financial PR will need proven literary ability and financial knowledge.

Career Development

You can seek employment in a company or government PR department or a consultancy and, after gaining experience, you can work freelance. Company employees can reach top management posts and, because there is a lot of mobility in this field, promotion prospects are good. Most people in PR switch jobs fairly often, especially at the beginning of their career. In mid-career they might move into marketing (see Chapter 11) or advertising and then set up their own PR business.

Job Opportunities

There are PR jobs in towns and cities all over the UK. The few vacancies that occur are advertised in the quality press and the trade press.

Starting Salaries

Starting salaries for graduate trainees are in the region of £7500.

Entry Requirements and Training

There are a few junior support posts for those with O levels (or equivalent) and consultancies occasionally offer traineeships for holders of A levels (or equivalent). There are traineeships for graduates – the subject of the degree may not be important – and for those with qualifications or experience in design, printing, photography and advertising.

Most training is given on the job and trainees are often encouraged to work for the Communication, Advertising and Marketing Education Foundation (CAM) diploma in public relations.

Other Awards and Courses
MSc in Public relations, Stirling U
BTEC HND in Business and finance, Public relations specialism, Distributive Trades C
College-based Secretarial course, media marketing and PR specialism, Cambridge CFE

Professional Institutions

Institute of Public Relations, Gate House, St John's Square, London EC1M 4DH has five categories of membership: Honorary Fellow/Member, Fellow, Member, Associate, Student.
PR Consultants Association, 37 Cadogan Street, London SW3 2PR

Further Information

Careers in Marketing, public relations and Advertising (Kogan Page)
'Financial public relations' in *How to Get a Highly Paid Job in the City* (Kogan Page).
Chapters on public relations in *How to Get On in Marketing, Advertising and Public Relations* (Kogan Page)
(See also **Publicists**, p 91 and Chapter 16.)

Chapter 11
Marketing

Many people mistakenly believe that marketing is just a more socially acceptable word for selling, whereas it is, in fact, the whole complex operation of identifying, anticipating and satisfying customers' needs in an efficient and profitable way. Selling is only one element, albeit a very important one, of what has been called by the Institute of Marketing 'the marketing spectrum' or by Professor Borden of the Harvard Business School 'the marketing mix'. The other elements are: research, development, planning, branding, pricing, packaging, advertising, public relations (PR), storage, handling, distribution, after-sales service. Separate chapters have been devoted to advertising (9) and PR (10).

Marketing is currently one of the two most popular career areas for non-science graduates, particularly women, who generally excel in PR, marketing research and selling. There are, of course, openings in marketing for those with qualifications in arts, science and technical subjects, and you can rise to managerial level even if you possess few academic qualifications, provided you have had the right experience. It is also possible to move into marketing in mid-career. The three broad categories into which this career area is divided are consumer, industrial and services marketing.

Marketing Research

Before any product can be successfully launched, the market has to be researched, and it is the findings of the marketing researchers that guide the operations of the other members of the marketing team and shape the marketing strategy.

Researchers collect, record, analyse and interpret information about all the problems relating to the transfer of goods from producer to consumer and about actual or potential consumers, clients or customers.

The work breaks down into quantitative and qualitative research. The former yields statistical data, eg the number of people who use a biological washing powder, the proportion of the population that travels to work on public transport, the area of the country in which there are the most private swimming pools; the latter yields information on, for example, attitudes, preferences, purchasing practices. Quantitative research is usually carried out on large samples and qualitative research on relatively small ones and can involve in-depth group discussion or psychological tests.

Marketing research techniques are also used in areas other than marketing, eg the compilation of opinion polls or the generation of social statistics, and it is possible to specialise in one of these kinds of work or in a particular kind of market-related study. You could become an expert in, say, awareness studying, which measures the effectiveness of manufacturers' messages, or in the study of special groups of consumers, such as doctors or farmers. For industrial research involving expensive pieces of equipment that are bought by professionals on the basis of performance, specifications and price, the researcher needs to have a thorough technical knowledge of the product and, in addition, an understanding of the structure of the industry involved.

What Goes into a Typical Marketing Research Survey?

The first stage is desk research: discovering and analysing information on the subject that has already been published or is stored in on-line databases. The second is field research among a representative sample of customers or potential customers, and there are a number of different data collection techniques. This is the activity with which most people are familiar; it is, in fact, the *market* research, a part of the wider activity of *marketing* research. In the *ad hoc* survey, face-to-face interviewing, telephone interviewing and mailed questionnaires can be used. For a continuous survey, where results are compared week by week or month by month, a panel has to be set up. It might be a panel of television viewers, whose viewing habits are recorded automatically by a meter attached to the back of a television set, or a consumer panel, whose members report by means of a diary or to an interviewer who calls at regular intervals. In the third stage, the findings are analysed, very often by computer, and in the fourth, they are interpreted, that is to say, the data are used in conjunction with variables, like market locations and seasonal fluctuations, to make informed and accurate predictions. The final stages are the compilation of the report and, possibly, its oral presentation.

Clearly, a marketing research consultancy needs people with an array of different skills and talents who are able to come together to form a team. The work demands an imaginative and conceptual approach – abstract projections about products and services which may not yet exist have to be related to concrete information – and the application of statistical principles. Furthermore, commissions have to be costed and carried out to a deadline.

In a small consultancy, which will probably undertake only *ad hoc* projects, the staff will tend to be generalists. In a large one, in addition to the managers, there will be executives, statisticians, computer programmers and data processors, field controllers, field interviewers, coding and editing clerks, graphics and production personnel and back-up staff. Such consultancies undertake *ad hoc* surveys and panel operations and their staff are specialists.

Consultancy market research executives oversee a project from start to finish. They analyse a client's problem and put forward a research proposal. If this is accepted, they design questionnaires and set up the data-gathering operation. When the data have been collected and processed, they analyse them, write up a report and frequently give an oral presentation.

The data gathering may be done by questionnaire, or it may be a matter of interviewing actual and/or potential clients/customers/consumers by telephone or face to face. Some manufacturing companies which have a marketing research department may be able to do their own data gathering, but consumer research necessitates thousands of interviews and is carried out by a consultancy which can call upon a field force or field department. A field controller – the great majority of them are women – recruits and trains interviewers, allots the work and collects the results. In the case of very large assignments the field controller will be assisted by a regionally based field supervisor. In a continuous assignment interviewers usually have a precise working brief, but in an *ad hoc* assignment they may have to exercise their own judgement on how to carry out the task.

Who Uses Marketing Research?

The different bodies which use marketing research – individual companies with a product or service to sell, financial institutions, trade associations, central and local government departments, social research bodies, political parties, business schools, avertising agencies, advertising media owners – may commission a survey/surveys or may have their own marketing research department. This means that if you were interested in, say, finance-related marketing research, you could look for employment at the head office of one of the clearing banks or with a research consultancy that specialised in financial work.

Personal Qualities

The work calls for the ability to analyse a client's problem, come up with a workable solution and present findings in a concise, clear manner. Marketing research executives should be able to communicate easily with all sorts of people as they must attract clients and may have to carry out research interviews. They need a good command of written and spoken English as findings may have to be presented orally as well as in a written report. In addition, they will have to design questionnaires and interpret statistics. Many surveys have to be done to strict deadlines, so market researchers should be able to work under pressure.

Interviewers need to be particularly skilled in dealing with people, many of whom will be reluctant to give either their time or their opinions.

Career Development

Promotion is on merit and those who perform well rise rapidly. A graduate recruit can reach the top of the research scale before the age of 30. Research executives can move into management, then directorhips. Some remain in marketing research and may set up their own business; others move into high-level posts in allied areas such as advertising or product development.

Job Opportunities

Numbers of vacancies are falling, consequently competition, which was always keen, is getting keener. Most of the consultancies are in or near London. Marketing research is an area where you can work part time and/or freelance and many freelances hire themselves to more than one organisation.

Vacancies are advertised in the quality press, the specialist marketing press, in such periodicals as *Campaign* and the *Economist*, in *IMRA News* circulated by the Industrial Market Research Association and in the Market Research Society's (MRS) *Newsletter*. The *Directory of Market Research Organisations* lists the consultancies; the MRS publishes *Organisations and Individuals Providing Market Research Services*.

Entry Requirements and Training

No formal qualifications are needed to enter marketing research, but many trainee or junior research posts are filled by graduates. Employers rarely stipulate particular degree subjects but statistics, economics, psychology, mathematics and sociology are relevant subjects, and a science or engineering degree would be useful preparation for industrial work. Marketing research is an option in many first and second degree courses and in business school courses. The Diploma of the MRS was introduced in 1973 and may become the accepted qualification for consumer researchers.

Graduate trainees receive most of their training on the job and it will include such subjects as: interviewing, questionnaire compilation, data analysis, report writing and presentation. Some companies send trainees on short introductory or subject-specific courses run by the MRS, the IMRA or the College of Marketing.

Many companies provide training for field interviewers, coders, editors and clerks, whose work usually requires simply a good educational background and common sense. However, such people can rise up the promotion ladder.

Other Jobs in Marketing

Sales and Sales Management
Personal selling is, perhaps, the best known and most visible marketing activity. For many people it provides the most obvious and direct way into a career in marketing and some experience of personal selling is normally required for a senior marketing post.

Broadly speaking, there are two kinds of sales staff: 'order makers' and 'order takers'. The former are engaged in industrial marketing; their products are usually expensive, complex items which the buyer will evaluate closely before deciding whether or not to purchase and order makers have to have a thorough technical knowledge of their product coupled with a grasp of their client's needs. Order takers work with strong advertising and promotional support, ie most commonly in the mass consumer market, and their work frequently includes giving help or advice with such matters as point-of-sale display. Order making, also called 'application selling', has a long selling cycle which may involve surveys, reports, recommendations and meetings before a sale can be made, whereas order taking, or 'action selling', moves quickly.

There are, in addition, specialised areas such as insurance selling, space and airtime selling (in newspapers, magazines, radio and television – see pp 24 and 112-13), service selling and know-how selling.

It is costly to keep sales staff on the road, so their performance is monitored and often their basic salary is small and they are expected to make up their earnings with commission payments.

Sales staff, though members of a marketing team, spend much of their time working on their own and the greater part of their day away from base. They have to plan their schedules carefully in order to maximise customer contact and minimise travelling time.

Career Development
Selling requires knowledge of both the product and the market and so few people go into it straight from school or college. Once you have acquired the necessary background knowledge, possibly by working in a laboratory or engineering workshop, or in a sales or customer service office, you can apply to be trained as a sales person.

Good sales staff are generally amply rewarded financially and for this reason many prefer to remain in sales rather than climb the management ladder. The first step up is often to the post of area manager and this can lead on, via national sales management, to the post of chief executive. Those interested in market planning or sales promotion can take a different path through, say, product management, market research or, perhaps, the management of a small division.

Product and Market Management
These are middle management activities. Product managers, who oversee and integrate all the activities that go into the successful sale of their product, are found in companies which produce a range of different products competing for the same end-use market, eg household cleaning products. They liaise with the production department to ensure

that adequate supplies of the product will be available and check that all the specifications – packs, sizes etc – comply with the specifications in the marketing plan, they co-ordinate the advertising and sales promotion, brief the sales force, check distribution and delivery schedules to ensure that they tie in with orders taken, and monitor consumer reaction and sales figures.

Market managers are found in companies whose products are destined for a range of different end-use markets, eg the food, clothing and cosmetics markets.

Both product and market managers carry a heavy burden of responsibility but lack the power to impose decisions on other functional managers; they have to combine the qualities of diplomat and leader. Those who do well can expect rapid promotion to senior management. Some companies recruit graduate trainees to fill product and market management posts; others promote their own clerical or sales personnel.

Distribution and Retailing

The exploitation of these two areas of marketing is just beginning. A company can make enormous savings by applying operational research techniques to inventory and transport problems and by computerising stock movement and sales. On the retail side, changes in shopping habits have resulted in 70 per cent of all retail purchases being controlled by fewer than 1500 buying points. Because of this concentration, retail organisations exercise enormous influence over production and marketing systems and offer interesting career opportunities.

International Marketing

The management functions of international marketing are very similar to those of domestic marketing. Obviously, the task of export sales personnel will vary according to the product or service they are selling. Some companies work through agents in the field; others, especially those selling plant or equipment, send their own staff overseas. Although English is the international language, fluency in a relevant foreign language could give anyone applying for an international marketing post an edge over other candidates.

Professional Bodies and Their Examinations

The Communication, Advertising and Marketing Education Foundation (CAM) (see p 115)

The Direct Marketing Centre, Millennium House, 21 Eden Walk, Kingston upon Thames, Surrey KT1 1BL. Examination: Diploma.

Industrial Marketing Research Association, 11 Bird Street, Lichfield, Staffordshire WS13 6PW, the professional association for people engaged in the search for and analysis of information relevant to the marketing of goods and services to corporate and institutional users.

Institute of Marketing, Moor Hall, Cookham, Maidenhead, Berkshire SL6 9QH, founded 1911 to develop knowledge about marketing, to provide services for members and registered students and to make the principles and practices of marketing more widely known and used throughout industry and commerce. The Institute has five categories of membership: Fellow, Member, Associate, Graduate, Registered student. Examinations: Certificate and Diploma.

Institute of Sales and Marketing Management, Georgian House, 31 Upper George Street, Luton, Bedfordshire LU1 2RD, has four categories of membership: Fellow, Member, Associate, Affiliate. Continuing professional training.

Institute of Sales Technology and Management Ltd, 4 Belvedere Road, Charminster, Bournemouth, has six categories of membership: Fellow, Member, Associate, Graduate, Affiliate, Registered student. Examinations: Intermediate Examination, Final Examination.

Management and Marketing Sales Association Examination Board, PO Box 6, Knutsford, Cheshire. Examinations: Intermediate Diploma in Selling, Standard Diploma in Selling, Higher Diploma in Sales Marketing, Advanced Diploma in Sales Management Diploma in Marketing Strategy and Management.

Market Research Society, 175 Oxford Street, London W1R 1TA, the professional body for those using survey techniques for market, social and economic research. Examination: Diploma.

Other Awards

University First Degrees
BA Combined Hons Marketing-French studies, BA Hons Art, design and marketing, Lancaster

MARKETING

BSc Hons Agriculture Agricultural and food marketing, Newcastle upon Tyne
BSc Hons Food science, food economics and marketing, Reading
BSc Modern languages and marketing studies, Salford
BA Hons Marketing, BSc in Technology and business studies, marketing and management science, Strathclyde.
BSc Single Hons Agricultural and food marketing, BSc Econ Hons Economics-marketing, Wales, Aberystwth

CNAA Polytechnic Degrees
BA/BA Hons Marketing (engineering), Textile marketing, Huddersfield
BSc/BSc Hons Marketing, Leicester
BA/BA Hons Fashion design with marketing, North East London
BA/BA Hons International marketing, Thames
BA Hons Retail marketing, Manchester
BA/BA Hons Business economics with marketing
BSc Hons Food marketing sciences, Sheffield

Higher Degrees awarded by Universities
MBA Marketing, City
MA, MSc Marketing, Marketing education; MPhil, LLM Marketing, Lancaster
MSc Agricultural economics-Agricultural marketing, London Wye College
MSc Marketing, Manchester
MSc/MPhil Marketing, International agricultural marketing, Newcastle upon Tyne
MA or MSc Marketing, Marketing and a foreign language, Salford
MSc Marketing, Strathclyde
MSc New product development, Ulster
MSc Agricultural and food marketing, Wales, Aberystwyth

Diplomas awarded by Universities
Postgraduate Diploma Agricultural marketing, Newcastle upon Tyne
Postgraduate Diploma Marketing, Marketing for industrialising countries, Strathclyde
Postgraduate Diploma Marketing, Ulster

Diplomas awarded by Polytechnics
Polytechnic Diplomas Marketing, Birmingham

Postgraduate Diploma Marketing, Bristol (CNAA)
CNAA Postgraduate Diploma, Marketing management, Liverpool
Polytechnic Diploma Marketing management, North East London
CNAA Postgraduate Diploma Marketing management, International marketing, North Staffordshire

BTEC HND in Business Studies
Marketing subjects may be taken as specialisms. Marketing is available at many colleges: Market research, Distributive Trades C; Languages and marketing, Bradford and Ilkley Community C, Bristol Poly, Lancashire Poly, Southampton CT, Buckinghamshire CHE; Export marketing, Southampton CHE; Purchasing and marketing, North London Poly; Marketing and advertising, Bristol Poly.

CNAA Diplomas
European marketing management, Buckinghamshire CHE
European marketing management, Napier Polytechnic, Edinburgh
Association of Business Executives: Advanced Diploma in Marketing, City Business C, Centre for Marketing and Management Studies, Greenwich C, London International C, West London C
British Direct Marketing Association: Diploma, Distributive Trades C
Institute of Commerce: Higher Diploma in Marketing, City Business C, Greenwich C
Institute of Commerce: Advanced Diploma in Marketing, City Business C
London Chamber of Commerce: Marketing (Higher), Aylesbury C, Distributive Trades C
Royal Society of Arts: Commerce (Marketing) Stage III, Thurrock TC

College Awards
Diploma in industrial marketing, Gwent CHE
Diploma in language and international marketing studies, East Devon CFE

Further Information

How to Get on in Marketing, Advertising and Public Relations (Kogan Page)

Chapter 12
Artist and Illustrator

Many people's idea of an artist is a smocked figure standing palette in hand before an easel, but that is not the kind of artist whose work will be outlined in this chapter. Art is very often bracketed with design (see Chapter 13); graphic designers need considerable artistic talent and creativity, and there are many jobs for artists where technique is as important as artistic creativity or originality.

Illustrators emerging from specialist illustration and/or graphic design courses may find full-time employment as illustrators/designers in publishing-house design departments where they might work on book jacket design or medical/scientific illustration, but most illustrators work freelance and their commissions come through personal contacts or through an agent.

There is a wide variety of work for illustrators including: book and magazine illustration, which may be anything from line drawing to full colour work; textbook illustration, which sometimes requires specialised knowledge; posters, which usually incorporate lettering; greetings cards; editorial illustrations for brochures and instruction manuals; board and other game illustrations.

Some illustrators, when starting out, apply for design jobs in order to gain work experience before going freelance; others do temporary or part-time work while building up their contacts. The degree or diploma show at the end of the course attracts many visitors who are on the look-out for new talent and first commissions often come this way. If you are going to make direct approaches to prospective employers you should prepare a carefully selected portfolio of your work. Many illustrators use an artists' agent to find them work, but agents can charge up to 25 per cent in commission. A list of artists' agents and their services is printed in the Association of Illustrators' *Survival Kit* (see p 136).

Personal Qualities

If you are going to do literary illustration you will need to be responsive to a writer's work and adaptable enough to fall in with his/her own conceptions of character and place. Greetings card work often calls for wit or humour. As most illustrators work freelance, they should possess some business sense.

Job and Career Prospects

In theory, illustrators can work anywhere in the country, but getting started in book or magazine illustration will be easier if you live within reach of the publishers so that you can go in and talk over a commission when it comes up. Once you have made a name for yourself – and to do this you will, of course, need to have talent and be reliable about meeting deadlines – you will find that those who commission work are prepared to take the time to send you possible jobs for your consideration. Working from home can be very lonely and some illustrators join up with others and rent a studio.

Entry Requirements and Qualifications

Theoretically, practising artists and ilustrators need have no academic qualifications, but most receive formal art training. Before taking a degree course, it is usual to complete a one-year, full-time art and design foundation course. (See p 140-41.)

Many of the courses listed below are in fine arts, ie art produced primarily for its aesthetic value; some will include instruction not only on the traditional skills of painting, drawing, engraving, sculpture etc, but also on print-making, photography, film and video. Check the content of the course you are interested in. If you want to take a degree course you will have to submit a comprehensive portfolio of your work. Most universities offering a fine arts course participate in the Joint Universities Portfolio Inspection Scheme (see *UCCA Handbook*). In Scotland, the four central (art) institutions co-operate in a scheme whereby students submit one portfolio to the college of their first choice. Applications to polytechnics and colleges of art should be made through the Art and Design Admissions Registry.

ARTIST AND ILLUSTRATOR

Courses and Awards

University First Degrees
BA combined Hons English-fine art, Exeter
BA Hons/Ord Design; Painting; Sculpture, Heriot-Watt
BA Hons Fine art, Leeds
BA Combined Hons Art (studio practice), London Goldsmiths' C
BA Hons Fine art, London UC
BA Hons Fine art, Newcastle upon Tyne
BFA Pass Fine art, Oxford
BA Hons Fine art; Art-design, Ulster

CNAA Polytechnic Degrees
BA/BA Hons Find art, Birmingham
BA/BA Hons Fine art, Brighton
BA/BA Hons Fine art, Bristol
BA/BA Hons Fine art, Coventry
BA/BA Hons Fine art, Duncan CA
BA/BA Hons Fine art, Glasgow
BA Hons Fine art, Kingston
BA Hons Fine art, Lancashire
BA/BA Hons Fine art, Leeds
BA Hons Fine art, Leicester
BA/BA Hons Fine art, Liverpool
BA/BA Hons Fine art, North East London
BA/BA Hons Fine art, Manchester
BA/BA Hons Fine art, Middlesex
BA/BA Hons Fine art Newcastle upon Tyne
BA Hons Fine art, North Staffordshire
BA/BA Hons Fine art, Manchester
BA/BA Hons Fine art, Robert Gordon's
BA/BA Hons Fine art, Sheffield
BA/BA Hons Fine art, Sunderland
BA/BA Hons Fine art, Trent
BA Hons Fine art, Wolverhampton

Higher Degrees awarded by Universities
MFA (Master of Fine Arts) Design; painting; sculpture; MSc Fine art, Newcastle upon Tyne
MFA Fine art, Reading
MA (RCA) Painting; sculpture; illustration, Royal C of Art

CAREERS IN THE MEDIA

MA Fine art, Ulster
MA Art; studio studies with art history, Wales Aberystwyth

Higher Degrees awarded by Polytechnics
MA Fine art, Birmingham
MA Fine art, Manchester

Diplomas awarded by Universities
Art and design, London Goldsmiths' C
HD in Fine art, London UC
Postgraduate diploma Art and design, Ulster

Diplomas awarded by Polytechnics
Postgraduate diploma Fine art and design, Edinburgh
GSA Postgraduate diploma Fine art, Glasgow
Polytechnic diploma Art and design, Lancashire
Polytechnic diploma foundation studies (Art and design), Liverpool
Polytechnic diplomas and certificates Art and design foundation studies; Art and design studies; Fine and applied art, City of London

Certificates awarded by Universities
Certificate Fine art, Exeter
Certificate foundation studies in Art and design, Ulster

Certificate awarded by Polytechnics
Certificate art, Brighton
CNAA postgraduate courses in art and design: the Council has approved a number of postgraduate studies for the award of MA. Approved courses in Find art are offered by Birmingham Poly, Chelsea, Goldsmiths', Manchester, Newcastle, South Glamorgan, Trent

Other Awards
The Royal Academy Schools
The Royal Academy of Arts, Burlington House, Piccadilly, London W1V 0DS
The RA Schools award the Royal Academy Schools' Postgraduate Diploma.

National Certificates and Diplomas
BTEC HND Illustration, Cambridgeshire CAT

BTEC HND Technical illustration, Bournemouth and Poole CAD, Cornwall CF&HE
SCOTVEC Diploma in Art/design, Glasgow CBP
SCOTVEC National Certificate modules/Diploma in Art/design Aberdeen C Com, Borders CFE, Cardonald C (Glasgow), Central C Com (Glasgow), Dumfries and Galloway CT, Glasgow CB&P, Falkirk CT
CNAA BA/BA (Hons) Fine Art, Glasgow SA
CNAA BA Art and design, Bradford and Ilkley Community C
CNAA Art/design/craft, Sunderland Poly
CNAA BA (Hons) Fine art, Norwich SA, Leicester Poly, Loughborough CA&D, Trent Poly, Brighton Poly, Canterbury CA, Camberwell SA&D, Central SA&D (London), Chelsea SA, Goldsmiths' C, Kingston Poly, Middlesex Poly, North East London Poly, St Martin's SA, Wimbledon SA, Newcastle Poly, Sunderland Poly, Lancashire Poly, Manchester Poly, Bath CHE, Bristol Poly, Exeter CA&D, Falmouth SA, Gloucestershire CAT, Birmingham Poly, Coventry Lanchester Poly, North Staffs Poly, Stourbridge CT&A, Wolverhampton Poly, Humberside CHE, Leeds Poly, Sheffield City Poly, Gwent CHE, South Glamorgan IHE
CNAA BA/BA (Hons) Fine art, Robert Gordon's IT (Aberdeen), Hertfordshire CA&D, Sheffield City Poly, Duncan of Jordanstone CA
CNAA BA (Hons) Fine art, Wimbledon SA, Winchester SA
CNAA BA (Hons) Fine art and critical studies, St Martin's SA
CNAA Diploma in print making, Brighton Poly
Heriot-Watt University: BA (Hons) Drawing and painting, Edinburgh CA
University of Edinburgh/College: MA (Hons) Fine art, Edinburgh CA
University of Exeter: BA (Hons) Fine art and a language, Exeter CA&D
University of Leeds: BA (Hons) Art and design, Bretton Hall C

There are hundreds of regional and college awards, many of which are listed in *Careers in Art and Design*, 5th edition (Kogan Page).

Professional Bodies

The Association of Illustrators, 1 Colville Place, London W1P 1HN is the professional body. It is concerned with all aspects of illustrating, provides advisory services and promotes illustrators' work. It also organises an annual exhibition of illustrators' work and its publications include a newsletter and *Survival Kit*.

Further Information

Always send a self-addressed stamped envelope.

Association of Illustrators, 1 Colville Place, London W1P 1HN
Careers in Art and Design (Kogan Page)

Chapter 13
Design

Design is a very wide field and no attempt is made in this chapter to give a comprehensive account of the whole range of careers it offers; only areas of design that might be of interest to those wishing to work in the media are included. There is a separate chapter (Chapter 12) on artists/illustrators.

Design involves creativity, technical expertise and problem solving. A designer is briefed by client or employer on what is wanted, how much money is available for the project and who the end-users will be, and must then come up with suggestions, sketches or models which he/she will discuss with the person initiating the project. The original concept may have to be considerably modified, so designers must be prepared to be flexible.

Graphic Design

Most graphic design work is two-dimensional, though packaging, exhibition and display work are three-dimensional. College-trained graphic designers can find work in design consultancies, in advertising agencies, with book and magazine publishers, with record companies, with television and film companies, with printers, with in-house design groups in industrial and commercial companies, in museums, art galleries and arts organisations, and they can specialise in book or magazine design, record sleeves, packaging, photography, audio-visual materials, technical graphics, display and exhibition design, or typography.

Design consultancies are independent firms; some employ several different kinds of designer – graphic, package, product, display, exhibition, textile, furniture, interior – and offer a complete range of design services; others specialise in, for example, purely graphic design or publicity services. It can be very stimulating to work in a consultancy because of the variety of the assignments. For example, one day you could be designing simple letterheads and the next working in a team on the problems of updating an international company's image. Sometimes there is a clear distinction between senior designers, who oversee a job from its conception to completion, and design assistants, who do the detailed work along the way.

Advertising agencies (see Chapter 9) are major employers of graphic designers and the larger the agency the more specialised the work is likely to be. In an agency, a designer is a member of the creative team and works alongside copywriters and photographers. Agency work can include television commercials, newspaper and magazine advertisements, posters, packaging, point-of-sale display, leaflets, brochures, prospectuses and catalogues.

Book and magazine *publishers* employ graphic designers as art assistants and art directors. The art director, working in consultation with the editorial staff, is responsible for the overall visual appearance of the book or magazine. He/she chooses appropriate typefaces, decides on page layout and cover design. If you want to go into publishing you should choose a design course that has a strong typographical element. Record sleeve design is a similar type of work to book jacket design.

Television, film and video companies offer extremely wide-ranging graphics work. Graphic designers, working with the production director and set designer, design and supervise the execution of title sequences, credits and other graphic programme material, which can include cartoon sequences, charts of all kinds and such things as documents used as props. The work may be done by hand, with printing equipment or with computers and it calls for great artistic creativity and a range of technical skills. Graphic designers are rarely appointed from among external applicants. Television, film and video company graphic design departments also employ photographers, photographic assistants and rostrum camera operators.

Graphic design assistants work under the designer on all forms of graphic design. They must be able to carry out instructions accurately and neatly and work without close supervision. Trainees are generally at least 21; they should have good colour vision and hold a degree or equivalent qualification in graphic design.

Graphic assistants produce a variety of typographic material; for example, credit captions or labels and carry out such tasks as operating caption generators.

Printers employ designers to do layout work, though a lot of design is now done by the typesetter using a computerised system with a visual display unit (see p 96).

In-house designers in an *industrial or commercial company* generally work with the advertising, commercial, PR or personnel departments, designing such things as brochures, catalogues, prospectuses, training aids and promotion material.

Museums and art galleries use graphic designers to design exhibition catalogues and do labelling etc.

Three-dimensional Design

This field includes product, interior and set and/or costume design for theatre (see p 48), films, video productions and television. Television set designers not only work on sets for plays; every television programme, from a panel game to a studio discussion, has a set which has been designed to create a certain ambience. Designers work with producers and directors, they must understand the technical processes of production and have a feeling for how the content of the programme should be interpreted visually. The work requires knowledge of the history of art and architecture. Many television and film sets are viewed in close-up and from different angles so a great deal of planning goes into them; designers have to take into account the positioning and movement of performers, props, cameras, camera cables, microphone booms and lighting. They usually construct a scale model of a set for use in programme/production meetings and produce simplified architectural drawings from which costings can be made. When a set design has been agreed, plans are sent to the workshop and construction begins. Television set designers almost invariably begin as assistant designers. Applicants for traineeships should be 21+ and hold a degree or its recognised equivalent in interior design, art and design, stage design or architecture.

Personal Qualities

Apart from their artistic skills and professional expertise, designers need flair and originality. They should, however, be prepared to be adaptable and to modify their original ideas to meet a client's or employer's requirements and to work within an agreed budget. Often they will be expected to visualise finished work from a very vague working brief.

Job Prospects and Career Development

There are design jobs to be found all over the country but competition is tough and you will need a good portfolio of work to show at any interview. In advertising, promotion can be rapid for those with artistic ability and plenty of ideas. Many designers, after a period of working in an agency or consultancy, during which time they gain experience and build up contacts, eventually go freelance or set up their own business.

Addresses of design consultancies and of professional designers are maintained by the Chartered Society of Designers (formerly the Society of Industrial Artists and Designers, SIAD), which also runs a staff vacancy service. A register of designers' services appears every month in *Design*.

Union Membership

For information about the Association of Cinematograph, Television and Allied Technicians, see p 41.

Entry Requirements and Training

You do not have to hold any qualifications in order to work as a designer, but few unqualified designers get very far.

Most practising designers took a one- or two-year foundation course followed by a degree course on leaving school. Foundation courses are offered by most colleges of art and other colleges with suitable facilities throughout the country. Enquiries and applications should be addressed direct to colleges, listed in *Design Courses in Britain*, available from the Design Council, 28 Haymarket, London SW1Y 4SU. Entry requirements for foundation courses vary; for some O levels (or equivalent) are enough, for others at least one A level (or equivalent) is needed. There will be an interview at which applicants show a portfolio of their work.

Degree courses (normally three-year and full-time) are run by universities, polytechnics, art colleges, colleges of higher education and certain other institutions. A wide variety of subjects and specialisations is on offer. There are too many to list; consult *Design Courses in Britain* and ask advice from a careers teacher or officer, who will help you pick one that suits your talents and interests. Applications for most courses in art and design (excluding those at colleges in Scotland) must be submitted

DESIGN

through the Art and Design Admissions Registry, Imperial Chambers, 24 Widemarsh Street, Hereford HR4 9EP. You are advised to obtain prospectuses from institutions to ascertain the correct method of application.

Most BTEC awards in art and design have the title 'Design' followed by the area of specialism. A full list of approved courses run at each college can be obtained from BTEC, Board for Design, Central House, Upper Woburn Place, London WC1H 0HH.

The SCOTVEC Diploma in Art/Design is a two-year full-time course. There are a number of options and the courses are offered at the Glasgow College of Building and Printing.

City and Guilds offer eight separate 'Creative Studies' certificates.

Professional Bodies

The Chartered Society of Designers, 29 Bedford Square, London WC1B 3EG offers four categories of membership: Fellow, Member, Associate and Diploma Member.

Further Information

Always send a self-addressed stamped envelope.

The Design Council, 28 Haymarket, London SW1Y 4SU
The Scottish Design Centre, 72 St Vincent Street, Glasgow G2 5TN

Careers in Art and Design (Kogan Page)
Design Courses in Britain (Design Council)
Guide to Courses and Careers in Art, Craft and Design (National Society for Education in Art and Design)

Chapter 14

Photography

This is not an overview of all career openings in still photography; rather, it is an outline of those that concern working in the media.

It is a mistake to specialise at an early stage; if your circumstances changed for the worse, you might need to be flexible. The freelance and general-purpose photographer, in particular, needs to be versatile in order to attract a variety of jobs. Few people go straight into working as a photographer; most start out as an assistant in a laboratory or a studio.

Advertising and Publicity

This competitive field is highly specialised and demanding. Most assignments go to esteemed photographers who have experience and a reputation in a particular field. The work calls for imagination, creativity and considerable technical knowledge. The subjects can be anything from a sausage to a South Sea island and the pictures may be used in a number of media, eg brochures, posters. The photographer has to shoot the product to the best advantage and choose an approach suited to the medium for which the photograph is intended.

Generally, an advertising agency will approach several photographers and invite them to tender for the work. The one chosen, while he/she will be expected to contribute original ideas, will have to work to the art director's brief.

Photographers in this field must be versatile – equally at home in the studio and on location. They may be expected to provide suitable props. Mail order photography is a branch of advertising work.

Fashion

Fashion photographers need the same technical expertise and facilities as general advertising photographers. They may have to employ or hire make-up artists and hair stylists as well as other staff. They can find their own models or use a model agency. Fashion photographers must have the knack of getting the best out of their models.

Advertising and fashion assignments frequently have to be carried out against the clock. Photographers in these fields generally start out as messengers or assistants in a studio and fashion photographers rarely employ untrained assistants. Once you start to do some photographic work you must begin compiling your own 'book' or portfolio and spend a lot of time showing it to art buyers in advertising agencies. Advertising and fashion photographers are paid by the day (anything from £200 to £1000).

Industrial

There is a considerable amount of work both for in-house and freelance photographers. In-house photographers may be expected to do a very wide range of jobs. In a large company there may be several photographers backed up by technical and darkroom staff. In a small company the photographer will operate very much like the general-practice photographer. The work could include general publicity, eg brochures and catalogues, and in a technical industry it could be part of quality control. Industrial work is generally very secure. Vacancies are advertised in the trade press or through photographic employment agencies. Salaries will vary from company to company.

General Practice

About half of all professional photographers are employed in general practice. These are the familiar high-street photographers and many have a shop attached to their studio. The nature of the work will depend on the location of the business. There will almost certainly be a lot of 'social' work, weddings etc, possibly advertising work for local companies and agencies and some press photography for the local newspaper; in an industrial town there could be a lot of industrial work, photographs for PR brochures etc.

Employment opportunities and promotion prospects will depend very much on the nature and size of the practice. In a large firm which does developing and printing there may be trainee posts and the possibility of becoming a photographer's assistant.

Educational Work

Museums often use a vast amount of photographic material for exhibitions etc. In a small museum a photographer might be expected to photograph exhibits and maintain a picture library.

Press Photography

Good press photographers need an eye for news. The most difficult thing they have to do is encapsulate a complicated situation in a single monochrome photograph. They usually start by working on a provincial newspaper and much of the work is of strongly regional interest and can become somewhat mundane. It is extremely difficult to make the transition from a regional to a national newspaper on which the work is much more 'news' oriented.

A press photographer with one of the nationals needs to be talented and highly resourceful. The work is taxing and can be dangerous; it involves unsocial hours but is relatively well paid.

Agencies

Agencies employ their own photographers but make extensive use of freelances. They will only consider applications from recommended photographers who have had appropriate experience.

Editorial

Editorial photography illustrates and accompanies information in magazines, periodicals and technical journals. Practitioners generally concentrate on a particular subject, eg motor bikes or cars. Sometimes this work is done by an in-house photographer but more often a freelance is hired. Editorial work is done to a brief but the brief is generally less rigid than an advertising brief.

Photojournalism

A photojournalist tells a story with pictures; the opportunities for this sort of work are very limited as nowadays magazines, which used to be big purchasers of this material, tend to use features which require little illustration. There are more openings in photojournalism in Europe and the USA.

Working Freelance

You should not underestimate the difficulty of establishing yourself as a freelance photographer. From the outset you may need expensive facilities and equipment and in the early days you will be secretary, telephonist, marketing manager, bookkeeper, darkroom assistant and photographer. You will have to decide whether to train at a college or learn through experience. Very few courses teach you how to overcome the difficulties of working freelance. And however good a photographer you are, you will not survive unless you have business acumen.

Non-photographic Work

Picture libraries and agencies keep large stocks of colour and black-and-white photographs which they sell on behalf of photographers. They employ secretaries, telephonists and specialist staff, eg printers. Publishers employ photographic editors whose job it is to choose photographs for books and periodicals and, occasionally, to commission photographs. Picture researchers are employed to find photographs, eg for a television programme. They need an excellent memory and a wide range of sources.

Professional Photofinishing
This work will probably become increasingly automated; however, there is still considerable scope for the artisan and craftsman. There is currently a shortage of skilled technicians and this growing industry offers good career prospects. At the moment there is no college course which is really of any use to those wishing to enter this work but many of the larger companies offer their own in-service training courses. The main specialisations are: processing, printing, inter-negative making, duping, copying, photocomping, retouching and dye transferring, mounting, encapsulating and heat sealing. Those skilled in these techniques can move into areas such as advertising work.

Career Development

There is no formal career structure and the earning power of photographers depends upon their reputation.

Job Opportunities

Jobs crop up in all parts of the UK, but the large advertising agencies with international accounts and the national dailies are concentrated in and around London. There is a growing demand for photographic work of all kinds but competition for jobs is very strong and you stand a better chance of finding work if you possess technical expertise as well as photographic skill. Jobs are advertised in: *British Journal of Photography*, *Broadcast*, the *Journalist*, *Professional Photographer*, *UK Press Gazette*, the quality press and relevant trade press.

Entry Requirements and Training

Formal academic qualifications are not usually required of those wishing to become photographers, but at an interview for a traineeship or assistant's post you will be asked to show a portfolio of your work.

Training is usually given on the job and some employers grant trainees time off to attend courses.

Press Photographers

The Proficiency Certificate in Press Photography of the National Council for the Training of Journalists (NCTJ) is awarded at the end of up to three years' provincial newspaper indenture and course attendance for trainee press photographers. Direct entry recruits to provincial newspapers need five GCE O level (or equivalent) passes, including English language, with certain exceptions in England and Wales, or three O levels (or equivalent) including English in Scotland. For the full-time one-year course in press photography, to be followed by two and a quarter years' indenture, the entry requirements are to be under the age of 20 and have one A level (or equivalent) and four O levels (or equivalent) including English language. Suitable applicants will be required to take a written test and, if successful, will be invited to attend a selection interview. The application form can be obtained from the NCTJ, Carlton House, Hemnall Street, Epping, Essex CM16 4NL (enclose a 9in × 4in sae). Richmond College, Sheffield is the NCTJ-accredited college offering training for press photographers. (See also pp 77-8.)

Press photographers in Scotland normally take a full-time course in photography at a college of further education in Glasgow or Edinburgh and then apply for work on a newspaper.

CNAA Polytechnic Degrees
BA/BA (Hons) Film video and photographic arts, Glasgow
BA/BA (Hons) Applied photography, film and television, Middlesex
BA Photographic studies, Napier
BA/BA (Hons) Photography, Trent

BTEC and SCOTVEC
BTEC and SCOTVEC validate photographic training courses. Colleges offering BTEC courses submit their syllabuses to BTEC; if they are validated, the course comes up to BTEC standards, but course content will vary, so you should make sure that a course meets your needs before applying for a place on it. SCOTVEC syllabuses conform to a nationally agreed policy and to a national minimum standard.

City & Guilds
744 Professional photography, 745 Scientific and technical photography, 750 (Pilot) Photography assistants, 923 Photography

College Awards
Manchester Poly: polytechnic certificate in printing and photographic technology
Richmond C, Sheffield: pre-entry course in press photography
There are numerous private courses, the best known of which is given at the Photographer's Place, Bradbourne, Ashbourne, Derbyshire, DE6 1PB.

The British Journal Directory of Photographic Education is the most up-to-date and comprehensive directory of photographic courses.

Representative Organisations and Professional Bodies

The Arts Council of Great Britain, 105 Piccadilly, London W1V 0AU will advise on careers and training, offers grants for photographic research and subsidises exhibitions by independent organisations.

The Association of Fashion, Advertising and Editorial Photographers (AFAEP), 9 Domingo Street, London EC1Y 0TA offers its members legal or ethical advice and will negotiate on their behalf. It keeps a register of individuals who offer services to photographers.

The British Association of Picture Libraries and Agencies (BAPLA), c/o PO Box 284, London W11 4RP was set up to allow communication within the trade and provide other services.

The British Institute of Professional Photography (BIPP), 2 Amwell End, Ware, Hertfordshire SG12 9HN is a qualifying organisation for UK members. It recognises over 30 different specialisations. It represents professional photographers' interests, disciplines members who behave unprofessionally, organises conferences, exhibitions, seminars and workshops. There are five non-corporate grades of membership and corporate membership. Its journal is the *Photographer*.

The Bureau of Freelance Photographers, Focus House, 497 Green Lanes, London N13 4BP publishes a monthly newsletter and operates an advisory service.

The Master Photographers' Association (MPS), 1 West Ruislip Station, Ickenham Road, Ruislip, Middlesex HA4 7DW is open only to full-time professional photographers. It runs seminars and training courses, offers special insurance rates, legal and accounting advice. Its monthly magazine is *Master Photographer*.

Royal Photographic Society (RPS), The Octagon, Milsom Street, Bath, Avon BA1 1DN has three degrees of membership and a number of special interest groups for members. It arranges lectures, seminars, exhibitions and workshops.

Further Information

British Journal of Photography (Henry Greenwood)
Careers in Photography (Kogan Page)
Running Your Own Photographic Business (Kogan Page)

Chapter 15
Arts Administration and Sponsorship Work

Arts Administration

This rewarding work – for example, managing a concert hall, arts centre, opera house, theatre, orchestra, festival, regional arts authority or entertainments section of a local borough – involves presenting the arts to the public. It involves organising events, budgeting, liaising with grant-giving or sponsoring organisations and with artists. In a large concern there will be a team of people working under the manager – accountants, lawyers, office, advertising, publicity, box-office and transport staff – but in a small concern one person (or a handful of people) will have to do everything and some of the work may be hard labour, eg moving chairs.

A national orchestra is controlled by a board and may employ between 10 and 12 people on the administrative side. The managing director is responsible for planning; budgeting; finding engagements by, among other things, maintaining good relations with promoters, record companies, film and broadcasting companies; and handling sponsorship. The work calls for knowledge of the orchestral repertoire and excellent organisational skills. The manager is generally backed up and assisted by an administrator. The concerts manager liaises with promoters, arranges rehearsals, books halls and sees to it that conductor and players know exactly where to go and when. The personnel manager's job is very important, because many of the UK orchestras are made up of players who have to be booked for each engagement, and it calls for an excellent knowledge of the scoring of orchestral works. The personnel manager attends all rehearsals and concerts and, if there is no stage manager, may be required to put out chairs, music stands and music.

An opera or a ballet company is generally based in its 'house' or theatre. The managing director's job is similar to that of the orchestral manager. Permanent house and behind-the-scenes staff do work that is comparable to that done by their opposite numbers in the theatre (see Chapter 3).

There has been a huge increase in the number of festivals in the UK.

Few of them, however, keep their offices open all year round. The festival director is responsible for overall planning and for finding funding. Shortly before the festival begins the director has to hire such people as box-office staff, ushers, stage managers and transport personnel and, when the festival is on, supervise them.

The Arts Council is the largest patron of the arts in the UK. Each major arts discipline is represented by a team of specialised officers who advise committees on the allocation of funds. There are separate councils for Scotland and Wales. The Council subsidises theatre, opera and ballet companies; contemporary music; jazz; art and photography galleries; literary magazines and arts centres and gives grants to individual artists, composers and writers.

Regional arts associations in England and Wales are supported and financially assisted by the Arts Council and also by local authorities, industry and trusts. They encourage, advise and subsidise those who promote arts events in their region.

Local authorities control many of the new arts centres which are sometimes multi-purpose places of entertainment. The larger arts centres are closely concerned with the presentation of professional performances and many local authorities employ their own arts officers.

The British Council provides countries abroad with representative aspects of British arts. The London office has a small staff responsible for providing practical help and occasionally funding for individuals, orchestras and theatre companies wishing to tour overseas. There are Council staff based abroad who help co-ordinate the overseas tours of British artists.

Personal Qualities

Arts administrators need to be calm and practical and possess excellent powers or organisation. They must be able to get on with all sorts of people from international performing stars to removal men, and in the early stages of their career they should be prepared, when necessary, to roll up their sleeves and do practical jobs. The work calls for great attention to detail.

Job Opportunities and Career Development

Jobs in arts administration crop up all over the UK, wherever there are arts centres, concert halls or festivals. A good way to get started is to join a very small, informal team as a volunteer as it is much easier to find a career post if you have had some experience. Advertisements for paid posts appear in the quality press, the local press and in relevant arts publications.

Entry Requirements and Training
Arts administration is a field in which experience is as important as formal educational qualifications and knowledge of the art you would like to administer is practically indispensable. For example, orchestra managers have often been players and/or have a music degree/diploma.

Courses and Awards
MA Arts administration, MA Arts management in education, MA Librarianship and arts administration, MA Museum and gallery administration, MA Arts criticism, Diploma in arts administration, short in-service training courses, City U, Department of Arts Policy and Management
MSc/MBA Arts management, Durham U Business S
BA Performing arts (Arts administration option), short in-service training courses, Leicester Poly S of Performing Arts
MA Creative arts management, short in-service training courses, Newcastle Poly Faculty of Art and Design
Diploma in Arts administration, Roehampton IHE Drama Department
Diploma in Leisure and amenity management (Arts administration option), Institute of Leisure and Amenity Management, Lower Basildon
Short in-service training courses for managers of small-scale professional theatre companies, Independent Theatre Council, London
Short in-service training courses to improve management skills for arts companies and community groups, InterChange Trust, London
Short in-service training workshops to develop management skills for arts organisations and community projects, Research Training Initiatives, Newcastle upon Tyne

Those wishing to take the examinations of the Institute of Chartered Secretaries and Administrators must have three O levels (or equivalent) and two A levels (or equivalent) or a BTEC/SCOTVEC national award in business studies or public administration.

Sponsorship

Sponsorship (mostly of sport and the arts) is widespread in the UK and increasing; you can be involved in this activity as a giver of funds, a receiver of funds or as a sponsorship consultant. Commercial, industrial and financial institutions give sums of money, often guaranteed over a period of, say, five years, to support sport and the arts and in return receive publicity about their involvement. Sometimes this may be just a mention on a programme, but if the sponsored event is of wide public appeal, eg a snooker championship, a concert or play in which prestigious artists/actors take part, there will be media coverage which would be worth many thousands of pounds if it were translated into advertising terms.

Sponsorship is not a philanthropic activity; it is an arrangement made by two parties for their mutual benefit and when large undertakings are involved both sponsor and sponsored may appoint full-time staff to handle the business. Sponsors usually consider sponsorship as a public relations activity (see Chapter 10), not advertising, and undertake it for what it can do for the corporate image and for this reason they are unlikely to back 'controversial' arts events or get involved with sports (sportsmen/women, teams) which receive a bad press. Those seeking sponsorship, eg orchestras, theatre companies, sports organisers, teams, need money as their box-office/gate receipts, even when houses/ grandstands are full, do not cover running costs, and they must present an attractive 'package' that will convince potential sponsors they will get value for their money.

There are now a number of sponsorship consultants who can provide expert advice for both sponsor and sponsored. For example, they can act as 'marriage broker' between potentially suitable parties (such as a polo team – polo is an expensive, minority sport – and a manufacturer of up-market leather goods, a youth orchestra and a company wanting to woo the younger market), tell would-be sponsors what they can realistically expect from a given outlay, and help those seeking sponsorship to present their case.

Personal Qualities
Sponsorship work calls for excellent communication skills and sound financial expertise.

Job Opportunities and Career Development
This is a new career area and one way to get started is to join a company PR department (see Chapter 10); another route would be through theatre management (see Chapter 3) or arts administration.

ARTS ADMINISTRATION AND SPONSORSHIP WORK

Entry Requirements and Training
A degree in business studies or PR qualifications would be good preparation for sponsorship work. Entrants will receive on-the-job training.

Further Information
Always send a self-addressed stamped envelope.

Arts Council of Great Britain, 105 Piccadilly, London W1Y 4SU
Arts Council of Northern Ireland, 181a Stranmillis Road, Belfast BT9 5DU
Scottish Arts Council, 19 Charlotte Square, Edinburgh EH2 4DF
Welsh Arts Council, 9 Museum Place, Cardiff CF1 3NX
British Council, 65 Davies Street, London W1Y 2AA

Administration: The Flexible Professional Career (Institute of Chartered Secretaries and Administrators)
Directory of Courses of Arts Managers (Arts Council)
Practical Sponsorship (Kogan Page)
Successful Sponsorship (Woodhead Faulkner)

Chapter 16
Agency Work

Very few writers, actors, musicians or models handle their own business affairs; most of them hire an agent to do it for them. Agents act in the best interests of their clients: negotiating their contracts and fees, finding them work (or someone who will publish or perform their work), handling their publicity, offering them professional advice and helping them to develop their careers. In return for these services, agents take a percentage (between 10 and 20 per cent) of their clients' earnings. Agent and client are dependent on each other and a close personal relationship often builds up between the two.

Agents work through a network of professional contacts, and for this reason you would find it almost impossible to set yourself up as an agent when you were just beginning your career. You need to gain experience, to learn judgement and to make your contacts. For example, many literary agents start out in publishing. If you are determined to go straight from school or college into agency work, you will have to try to find a clerical or personal assistant's post in a large agency and such posts are hard to come by.

Personal Qualities
Agents need very sound judgement. One of the most important decisions they have to make is whether or not to take a client on to their books. In the literary, musical and theatrical worlds where agents operate, everyone knows everyone else and an agent who tries to promote clients who do not do well soon loses credibility. These worlds are exceedingly competitive and agents have to keep themselves informed of what is happening in order to seize every opportunity to put forward one of their clients. Agents should also possess negotiating skills, legal expertise and business acumen. Those who do a lot of publicity work for their clients (arranging press conferences etc) need to be adept at handling the media and be able to write interesting press releases. A number of agents specialise in this kind of work. (See also p 91, **Publicist**.) Agent's clients can be 'difficult', eg sensitive, temperamental, moody or egomaniacal, so tact and patience are needed in large measure. In a big agency there

will be a back-up team of secretaries, receptionists, accountants and legal advisers; lone agents operating from one room have to perform all these functions themselves – it therefore helps to be well organised and methodical.

Job Opportunities
New agencies open up every year, most of them in or near London. Many of these are simply one person operating from home with a telephone and a filing cabinet. Jobs are seldom advertised and the rare vacancies are filled by headhunting or nepotism.

Career Development
People usually come into this work after gaining experience in some related field, and many people, after working in an agency, set up their own business.

Entry Requirements
You do not need any formal educational qualifications for agency work, but an agency must be registered with a local authority before it can operate. Anyone applying for a clerical post will be expected to have had a good general education and applicants for, eg accountants' or bookkeepers' posts, should of course, have the appropriate professional qualifications.

Literary Agents

Literary agents act as middlemen between authors and publishers, film, television and radio producers and theatre managers. They find a publisher (or producer) for an author's work and negotiate the best possible deal for their client. They deal with the publisher (or producer) on all matters that affect their client – the contract, manuscript delivery, follow-up titles, advertising, publicity and paperback rights – and obtain payments when they fall due, thus freeing the client from time-consuming business which he/she may well be unequal to or incapable of dealing with.

Literary agents are usually responsible for the sale of non-print media rights, an area in which few publishers are competent to work effectively. They may build up expertise in the sale of film, radio, video or television, rights or have arrangements with other agents who work exclusively in these fields.

Like publishers, literary agents tend to specialise in particular kinds of literature, eg romantic fiction or military history, but whatever their area they look for evidence of literary ability coupled with sales potential before they will agree to take on a new client. They do not automatically accept all authors who approach them; there is a limit to the number of clients for whom they can arrange a satisfactory service. The first thing they do is read an author's manuscript(s) and some charge a fee for doing this.

Literary agents are frequently very supportive of their authors: they evaluate their work, sometimes suggesting changes that might be made, come up with subjects for new works, and help them in their struggles with personal, financial and creative problems.

Publishers consult literary agents when they have a project in mind but no author, and foreign publishers may use UK literary agents when they want to bring out an English edition of a work already published abroad.

Agents who work exclusively for publishers are called scouts. They seek out new authors, manuscripts and information on books published abroad. They need wide contacts in the international publishing field. A scout based in a foreign country needs a good working knowledge of the language of that country in order to be able to scan new literature. Film and television companies commission scouts to look out for books that would transfer to the small or large screen.

Professional Body

The Association of Authors' Agents is the trade association of UK literary agents. Members agree to observe a code of practice in the conduct of their business.

Further Information

The Association of Authors' Agents, 49 Blenheim Crescent, London W11 2EF
Careers in Publishing (Kogan Page)
Writers' and Artists' Yearbook (A & C Black)

Model Agents

Model agents act as middlemen between their clients and the photographers or fashion designers/houses that require a particular type of model for an assignment. Model agents will sometimes accept promising models who have had no training or experience, and take them in hand themselves, sending them to a good hairdresser, putting them in touch with cosmetic agents and teaching them how to hold a pose for photographic work or to make the basic walks and turns for showroom or catwalk modelling. Often, they build up a close, almost parental, relationship with young clients, for example, helping them to organise their finances, passing on health and fitness tips, advising them, when necessary, to have teeth crowned or straightened and suggesting what pieces of basic modelling equipment they should buy.

They act for their clients by setting up the arrangements for an assignment, negotiating the fee and making sure this is paid, and keeping a record of assignments.

Most model agencies are located in London; there are a few in other parts of the UK, and their names and addresses can be obtained from local authorities. Bona fide agencies never advertise – they do not have to as they receive hundreds of applications from models trying to get on to their books. Some take on a broad range of clients, some specialise, eg in black, middle-aged or even ugly models.

Professional Body
Many of the most reputable and well-known agents belong to the Association of Model Agents, which will supply a list of the names and addresses of all the agencies it guarantees.

Further Information
The Association of Model Agents, The Clockhouse, St Catherine's Mews, Milner Street, London SW3 2PU
Careers in Modelling (Kogan Page)

Theatrical Agents

Most actors, dancers, directors and choreographers hand over the business of finding work and negotiating contracts to an agent. There are a few really big agencies with large staffs and hundreds of clients; these have different departments handling theatre, film and television contracts and are sometimes impersonal. The ones which manage the big names get to know of forthcoming productions well in advance and so have the chance to suggest some of their unknown clients for smaller parts; frequently they have close links with management. The smaller agencies offer their clients more personal attention and often get to know them well and take pleasure in helping to shape their careers. There are one or two individual agents who rely on their flair and contacts and undertake to place a few hand-picked clients.

Theatrical agents are always on the look-out for new talent and attend the end-of-course productions put on by the major drama schools. Agents not only try to find work for their clients, they negotiate their fees and contracts, ensure that they get proper billing and give them professional advice, which might occasionally involve telling them to turn down a part that could harm their image.

Further Inforation
Careers in the Theatre (Kogan Page)

Agents who handle Musicians

Concert Agents
Concert agents look after the interests of classical musicians; they may spend quite a lot of time visiting concert promoters and opera managers at home and abroad in order to 'sell' their clients. When they arrange an engangement or tour, they negotiate contracts and fees, see that their client gets adequate billing, make hotel bookings, travel arrangements, meet the client at the airport, attend the concert and fend off (or discreetly encourage) the press.

They listen to as many young musicians as they can and learn to spot potential. A musician at the start of a career needs guidance from an agent on which engagements to accept; for example, a singer who takes on a heavy role before his voice is ready for it can harm himself both physically and artistically.

Most agents start off in established agencies learning the concert and opera circuit.

Professional Body
The British Association of Concert Agents (address below)

Further Information
The British Association of Concert Agents, 12 Addison Park Mansions, Addison Gardens, London W14 0BE
British Music Yearbook
Careers in Classical Music (Kogan Page)

AGENCY WORK

The Pop Music World
In the world of pop music things are different and there is work for managers, agents and promoters.

Managers
Many people start off managing a group of friends; for example, they join a group as the fifth member of a four-piece band and arrange the bookings, promotion and publicity, tour with the group and take one-fifth of any proceeds that result from their negotiations.

Further up the ladder, experienced managers, who have built up contacts within the industry, scout for talent and will take on a group that they consider has potential, hoping that one day they will be able to build it up into a big name. Manager and group work out a 'marketing plan' together and then the manager sets out to generate as much excitement as possible around the group – the ultimate aim, of course, being to land a recording contract.

Once an act has begun to make a name in the pop music world a manager has to keep alive, and generate new, interest in it, making sure that it is not over-exposed or over-worked.

Music Agents
Music agents deal with the 'live' interests of pop musicians, running their tours in the UK and abroad. The work calls for organisational skills as it involves booking a venue, renting trucks (with experienced drivers), renting sound and lighting equipment (with an experienced crew to set it up and use it), erecting a stage (which may need elaborate scenery), hiring security men and a tour manager, arranging advertising and advance publicity. Nowadays, there are not many music agents as fewer and fewer musicians go on tour; the costs and risks of touring are considerable and musicians get a better financial return and more exposure from an expensive promotional video.

Many agents, before setting up in business, ran college social events. They then started working professionally from home, managing the live interests of acts too small to engage the interest of the big agents. Nearly all small agencies soon go out of business but those agents who have managed to book their acts into venues for break-even fees and organise contracts efficiently usually find work in one of the big companies.

Promoters
They hire a venue, be it a local club or Wembley Stadium, and find the

acts to fill it. They need to possess organisational skills and business acumen.

Further Information
Careers in the Music Business (Kogan Page)

Chapter 17
Information Gathering and Handling

This is a very varied field; it suits specialists and generalists, for it can cover any and every subject.

Library Work

It is a long time since the word 'library' was used simply to describe a collection of books or other reading matter; there are now slide, film, picture, map, disc, tape, video and other sorts of collections which are classified, catalogued and kept for reference or borrowing, and the people who manage them are called librarians. If you intend to go into traditional library work, you will need to be trained and to acquire professional qualifications, but if you wish to be, say, a film or video librarian in a broadcasting organisation, you might not need library qualifications but you would need a knowledge of production and storage techniques and your duties could include simple editing.

Librarians collect, organise, display and make available materials for library users. They have to keep abreast of new material, decide what to order (this will involve taking into consideration such matters as storage space and budget apportionment), catalogue and classify acquisitions as they come in, and check stock. Almost everyone involved in library work has to be familiar with computerised information storage and retrieval techniques, microfiche and microfilm. Librarians often put new materials on display or inform library users about them by circulating lists or bulletins which may contain abstracts. Library users may need only to be told where the material they require is stored and they will do their own information gathering, but sometimes librarians have to deal with enquiries that take hours, if not days, of research. The librarian who is in charge of a specialist collection, eg economics literature or classical records, will need degree-level knowledge of the field. The librarian in industry or commerce may be expected to run a reference, enquiry, abstracting and translation service for members of the organisation, to provide them with up-to-date information related to their work, and to store, and have readily available, literature produced by the organisation itself.

In a large library there will be a staff consisting of qualified librarians and library assistants. The latter will probably receive on-the-job training and may be encouraged to study part time for professional qualifications. Their duties are generally a mixture of library and clerical tasks; for example, they process acquisitions, issue material to users, shelve new and returned items and check that such things as periodicals arrive regularly.

Information Science

Information scientists (also called information officers) do work that is similar to traditional library work; that is to say, they collect, store and make available material for reference or loan, but as they tend to serve the needs of specialists, eg engineers or R and D personnel, they themselves must possess degree-level specialist knowledge and an important part of their work is information evaluation. Nearly all information scientists are graduates and company information scientists may work closely with staff in training and/or publicity departments. For the former they might provide illustrative material for training courses and for the latter edit or prepare press handouts.

Work Settings

Almost half the trained librarians in the UK work in public libraries and over 20 per cent in institutes of further and higher education, but these are not the work settings that will interest the reader of this book. If you want a career in the media you will be looking for a librarian's (or information scientist's) post in a picture library, broadcasting organisation, advertising agency, a large or medium-size public or private company, a newspaper or publishing group.

Media work has to be done to strict deadlines (newspapers go to press and radio and television programmes go on the air and cannot be late) so you must be able to work fast and accurately under pressure. If you were employed in a broadcasting organisation, most of your work would be related to programme production. For example, a music or record librarian would be expected not only to retrieve material for those making or presenting programmes, but to come up with suggestions for such things as signature tunes or background music.

Personal Qualities

Librarians and information scientists need a methodical approach to their work, an enquiring mind and a good memory. They usually enjoy using the tools of the trade: catalogues, reference books, on-line data systems etc and take pleasure in tracking down obscure pieces of information required by users. A good service will be much appreciated and heavily used.

Job Opportunities

Over the past ten years there has been a big increase in the number of people employed in information handling, but the demand for information specialists has now peaked. Competition is stiff in all fields; more people are chasing fewer jobs because institutions of further and higher education and public libraries have been forced to cut their budgets, and trained graduate librarians are accepting non-professional posts.

Jobs are to be found in all parts of the UK and vacancies are advertised in the *Times Literary Supplement*, the *Listener*, the quality press, the *Library Association Record*, or the *Library Association Vacancies Supplement*.

Career Development

It is hard to predict how the career of librarians working outside the public library system might develop. Any BBC employee can apply for a transfer under the Corporation's attachment scheme (see p 28). Company employees may be able to rise to managerial posts or can enhance their prospects by moving to larger firms offering more scope. Information scientists can move into information broking or consultancy and can set up their own business.

Starting Salary

About £7300 for a qualified librarian or information scientist, about £4000 for a library assistant.

Entry Requirements and Training

Librarianship is a graduate profession. You must have a degree in librarianship, or have a degree in another subject and successfully complete a postgraduate course approved by the Library Association (LA), and in some cases practical experience is required.

The LA keeps a register of chartered librarians. Chartered status is awarded to those who successfully complete an approved first degree or postgraduate course and have had the requisite three years' experience and practical training.

Library assistants do not have to hold professional qualifications but will be expected to have A level (or equivalent) passes. There is a BTEC National Award: Double Option Module in Librarianship and Information Work; a SCOTVEC HNC in Library and Information Science; and a City and Guilds Library and Information Assistant's Certificate No 737.

Information science is also a graduate profession. You must have a degree in information science, or in a relevant discipline and successfully complete a postgraduate course in information science or information studies.

Courses and Awards

University First Degrees
BSc Communication and information studies, Brunel
BSc Hons Information engineering, Lancaster
BA Library studies and English/geography/history; BA Library studies; BSc Library studies/mathematics/social science/PE and sports science, Loughborough
BS Hons Librarianship; BSc (Pass) Information engineering, Strathclyde
BLib (joint Hons) Librarianship and law, Librarianship with approved arts/science/social science subject, Wales, Aberystwyth

CNAA Polytechnic Degrees
BA/BA Hons Librarianship and information studies, Birmingham

BA/BA Hons Library and information studies, Brighton
BA/BA Hons Librarianship; BSc (Hons) Information science, Leeds
BA/BA Hons Librarianship and information studies, Liverpool, North London
BA/BA Hons Library and information studies, Manchester, Newcastle upon Tyne
BA Librarianship and information studies, Robert Gordon's

Higher Degrees awarded by Universities
MLS Library studies, Belfast
MA Librarianship and arts administration; MSc Information engineering; City
MA and MA (Collegiate) Bibliography, publishing and textual studies, Leeds
MArAd Archive administration, Liverpool
MA Library and information studies, Archive studies, UC London
MA, MSc, MTech, MLS Library and information studies, Archives, Library studies and information, School librarianship, Loughborough
MA Librarianship; MPhil (Educational studies) Librarianship, Sheffield
MSc Information and library studies, Strathclyde

Higher Degrees awarded by Polytechnics
MA Librarianship, Leeds

Diplomas awarded by Universities
Library and information studies, Belfast
Diploma Library and information studies, Archive studies, UC London
Postgraduate diploma Information and library studies, Strathclyde
Postgraduate diploma Archive administration, Wales, Bangor
Diploma Archive administration, Librarianship, Diploma in educational librarianship, Wales

Diplomas awarded by Polytechnics
CNAA Diploma in Professional studies school library and information studies; CNAA Postgraduate Diploma Librarianship and information studies, Birmingham
Diploma in librarianship and information work, Leeds
CNAA Postgraduate Diploma Librarianship and information studies, Liverpool
CNAA Postgraduate Diploma Librarianship, Manchester

Postgraduate Diploma Information and Library services, Newcastle upon Tyne

Certificates awarded by Universities
Pre-diploma Archive administration, UC London

BTEC and SCOTVEC
BTEC NC in Business and finance, Library and information work option, Southgate TC
BTEC ND in Public administration (Library and information studies), Loughborough TC
SCOTVEC NC Modules, Library and information science, Telford CFE, Edinburgh, Aberdeen C Com, Central C Com, Glasgow
SCOTVEC Certificate in information science, NC Modules, Kirkcaldy CT
SCOTVEC HND in Information studies, Bell CT, Hamilton, Dumfries and Galloway CT, Falkirk CT, Kirkcaldy CT, Queen Margaret C, Edinburgh, Scottish C of Textiles, Galashiels

City and Guilds
C&G 737 Library and information assistants is available throughout the UK.

College Awards
Certificate in media resources, South Thames C
Diploma in library studies, Nene C, Northampton

College-based Courses
Foundation studies in librarianship, Leeds Poly
Pre-professional library work, South Trafford CFE

Professional Institutions and Associations

The Library Association, 7 Ridgmount Street, London WC1E 7AE has two categories of membership: Fellow and Associate, and a qualifying examination. Courses of study approved by the LA are available at: Robert Gordon's IT, College of Librarianship Wales, Aberystwyth, The Queen's University of Belfast, City of Birmingham Polytechnic, Brighton Polytechnic, University of Strathclyde, Leeds Polytechnic, Liverpool Polytechnic, Ealing CHE, Polytechnic of North London,

University College London, The City University, Loughborough University of Technology, Manchester Polytechnic, Newcastle upon Tyne Polytechnic, University of Sheffield.

The Institute of Information Scientists, 44 Museum Street, London WC1A 1LY has four categories of membership: Fellow, Honorary Fellow, Member, Affiliate.

Further Information

Always send a self-addressed stamped envelope.

Association of Information Management (ASLIB), 26-27 Boswell Street, London WC1N 3JZ

Scottish Library Association, Motherwell Business Centre, Coursington Road, Motherwell

Careers in Librarianship and Information Science (Kogan Page)
Information Work as a Career (ASLIB)

Chapter 18

Administration and Back-up Work

You may like the idea of working in the media but imagine that this whole area is closed to you because you are not creative or artistic. You would be wrong to think like this; there are plenty of interesting media jobs for those with professional qualifications or training.

Accountancy, Bookkeeping and Other Financial Work

Accounts departments of advertising agencies, literary (and other) agencies, broadcasting organisations, design consultancies, film production companies, newspapers, industrial and commercial companies, printing firms, PR consultancies, publishing houses and large theatres recruit professional accountants, bookkeepers, trainees and juniors.

The financial work includes: preparing and controlling long- and medium-term company and departmental budgets, providing financial reports and audits, supervising wage, salary and expense payments and managing pension funds. In a broadcasting organisation, film production company or theatre there will also be work directly connected with programmes and/or productions. Accountants provide management with information on the state of programme or production budgets and estimate and monitor production costs. They often work closely with directors and need a thorough knowledge of how programmes or films are made and plays produced.

Royalties clerks in a publishing house, literary (or other) agency, record company, theatre, or broadcasting organisation have accounts training and generally have work experience. They need to understand the terms in contracts as they relate to payments due to authors, musicians, actors and other artists. Royalties clerks receive notification of all sales and performances etc and credit the relevant accounts with the sums due. Royalties are usually paid twice a year and payment time is a period of intense activity.

In a printing firm the estimator and costing clerk need knowledge of printing processes and financial training or experience. Estimating is responsible work as mistakes are likely to be costly and may not be discovered until it is too late to do anything about them. The costing clerk itemises all expenses on the customer's bill.

Accountants and bookkeepers need professional expertise and a thorough knowledge of the field in which their organisation is engaged. Accountants need not spend their entire professional life in an accounts department; the present Director General of the BBC started out as an accountant.

Administration

There are administrative posts in any large organisation and the people who occupy them are concerned with such matters as purchasing, central services, transport and personnel. Personnel work involves recruiting, training, job grading, salary administration, record keeping and industrial relations and has its own professional training.

Data Processing

Computers are used for such tasks as stock and cost control, cataloguing and statistical analysis. Computer departments recruit data preparation operators, computer operators, systems analysts, programmers and technical and support staff.

Legal Work

There is a great deal of work connected with contracts and copyright in broadcasting organisations, literary (and other) agencies, publishing houses and record companies. Work in a contracts department demands a thorough knowledge of contract, copyright, employment and trade union laws and legislation. Other fields in which legel expertise is required include video piracy, classification, data protection, libel laws and court reporting.

Secretarial and Clerical Work

There is an exceedingly wide range of jobs for secretaries and clerks in the media. The work is usually interesting and can provide a rewarding career in itself. However, many people look on secretarial posts as a spring-board to more demanding senior jobs and for this reason a lot of graduates apply for secretarial posts. There is much to be said for seeing what goes on in an organisation, learning the ropes and, above all, being on the spot when the right opportunity crops up. Secretaries may work for one person or for several, alone or in groups. They need accurate shorthand (80/100 wpm) and typing (30/40 wpm), good educational qualifications, common sense, initiative and a good telephone manner.

Clerks do such jobs as handling mail, photocopying, printing and filing. Those who can type (30/35 wpm) or have an aptitude for figures have more opportunities open to them. (See also **news typist**, p 22)

Statistical Work

Statisticians can find work in advertising, broadcasting and marketing research. Advertising agencies employ statisticians in the media planning department. Broadcasting organisations employ statisticians to carry out audience research. In a small market research consultancy staff tend to be generalists and statisticians may be called upon to perform such tasks as compiling questionnaires, liaising with clients and presenting findings, whereas in a large consultancy staff usually do specialist work.

Job Prospects

Unlike many who work in the media, administration and back-up staff are generally salaried employees and, therefore, enjoy job security. Work is available all over the UK and jobs are advertised in the quality press and the trade press.

Entry Requirements and Training

Administration and back-up staff will be expected to be professionally trained; however, additional on-the-job training will be provided for those whose work calls for special skills or knowledge.

Index

Accountancy work 168–9
Acquisitions editor 84
Actor 55–63
Administration 168–71
Advertisement sales 90
Advertising 110–16, 138
   agencies 138
   photography 142
Agency work 154–60
Announcer 17
Application, letter of 9–10
Armourers 51
Artist/Illustrator 131–6
   and see Design
Arts administration 149–51
Assistant, director (film/video) 38
Audio work, *see* Sound operator 25

BBC 27–8
Book production 87–8
Boom handler, *see* Sound personnel 9
Box office manager 50
Broadcasting 17–34, 73, 106
   see also Radio, Television

Camera operator 18, 38
Carpenters and joiners 51
Casting director 47–8
Choreographer 64–5
Clerk 170
Columnist (newspaper) 71–2
Commissioning editor 84
Concert agent 158
Continuity 37
Copyright and permissions editor 86
Correspondent (newspaper) 72
Costume designer 18
Craft posts 18, 51
Critic 72

Curriculum vitae 10–11

Dancer 64–5
Data processing 169
Design 137–41
   (periodicals) 90
Designer:
   (theatre) 48–9
   (publishing) 88
Desk editors 85
Director:
   (film/video) 37
   (programme) 23
   (theatre) 47
Disc jockey, *see* Music presenter 21
Distribution:
   (marketing) 127
   (periodicals) 90
Dresser 19
Dressmaker 19
Dubbing mixer, *see* Sound personnel 39

Editor:
   (book publishing) 84–6, 91, 92
   (broadcasting) 18
   (film) 39
   (newspaper) 72
   (periodicals) 89
Editorial assistant 85, 89
Education officer 51
Electrician 19
Employee/freelance 8
Engineer (broadcasting) 20

Fashion photography 142–3
Feature writer 72
Film assistant, *see* Projectionist 23
Film editor 39

INDEX

Film industry 35–45, 57, 106, 138
Film processing 40
Floor manager (broadcasting) 20
Freelance/employee 8

Graphic design 137, 138

Hairdresser, 52, 53
House manager 50

Independent broadcasting employers 28–30
Indexing 91
Industrial photography 143
Information gathering and handling 161–7
Information science 162
International marketing 127
Interview 10–11

Journalism 71–81

Legal work 169
Lexicography 92
Librarian 161
Library work 161–2
Lighting cameraman/woman 38
Lighting director 21, 50
Lighting electrician, see Electrician 19
Literary agent 155–6

Magazines, see Periodicals
Make-up artist 52
Marketing 21, 88, 121–30
Marketing research 121–4
Media personality 69
Model 66–8
Model agent 156–7
Model maker, see Visual effects designer 27
Museums and art galleries 139, 144
Music business 159–60
Music presenter 21
Musician 66

News typists 22
News work 22
Newspapers 71–3, 77–8, 105, 112

Performers 55–70
Periodicals 73, 78–9, 89–91, 105, 112
Personnel work, 169
Photofinishing 145
Photographic modelling 67
Photography 138, 142–8
Photojournalism 144–5
Picture libraries 145
Picture research 86–7, 145
Plumber 51
Presenter (broadcasting) 22
Press agencies 74
Press officer 51
 and see Public relations
Press photography 146
Press service 74
Printing 96–103, 138
Producer:
 (broadcasting) 22
 (film/video) 36–7
 (theatre) 46
Product manager 126–7
Production assistant:
 (broadcasting) 23
 (publishing) 87
Production controller (publishing) 87
Production director (publishing) 87
Production manager (film/video) 37
Production staff (theatre) 51
Programme director 23
Projectionist 39
Property staff 52
Public relations 117–20
Publicist 91
 and see Public relations
Publicity officer 51, 88
Publishers' reader 92
Publishing 82–95, 138

Radio 57, 73–4, 79, 113
 and see Broadcasting
Reporter (newspaper) 71
Researcher 24
Retailing 127
Rights editor 85, 86
Rostrum camera operator 138
Runner (film industry) 40

INDEX

Sales 24, 88, 125–6
  and see Advertisement sales
Sales staff 24, 88
Scenic artist 51
Script editor (broadcasting) 25
Script girl, *see* Continuity 37
Secretarial and clerical work 40, 170–71
  and see News typists 22
Set designer 48
Setting assistant, *see* Stagehand 25–6
Sound manager 50
Sound mixer, *see* Sound personnel 39
Sound operator 25
Sound personnel (film/video) 39
Sound recordist, *see* Sound personnel 39
Sponsorship 151–3
Stage manager 26, 49
Stagehand 25–6
Statistical work 170
Studio manager 26
Stunt performer 63–4
Sub editor (newspaper) 72

Technical assistant, *see* Engineer 20
Television 57, 73–4, 79, 113, 138
  and see Broadcasting
Television recording operator 26
Television set designer 138
Theatre 46–54, 106–7
Theatre manager, *see* House manager 50
Theatrical agent 157–8
Three-dimensional design 139
Translation 107
Transmission controller 26
Typesetting 96–7

Union membership 11–12, 41, 55, 66, 77

Video industry 35–45, 138
  and see Film industry
Vision mixer 27
Visual effects designer 27

Wardrobe work 52
Writing 72, 104–9